Social Choice and
Multicriterion
Decision-Making

Social Choice and Multicriterion Decision-Making

Kenneth J. Arrow and
Hervé Raynaud

The MIT Press
Cambridge, Massachusetts
London, England

This book was set in Palatino by Achorn Graphic Services, and printed and bound by Halliday Lithograph in the United States of America.

Library of Congress Cataloging-in-Publication Data

Arrow, Kenneth Joseph, 1921–
 Social choice and multicriterion decision-making.

 Bibliography: p.
 Includes index.
 1. Social choice—Mathematical models.   2. Decision-making—Mathematical models.   I. Raynaud, Hervé.
 II. Title.
 M271.A73   1986   302'.13   85-19913
 ISBN 0-262-01087-9

Contents

Contents

Social Choice and Multicriterion Decision-Making

Introduction

The current models used in operations research for the multicriterion ranking of a finite set of alternatives often lack firm (mathematical) foundations. This book intends to derive, from the lessons of social choice theory, possible foundations for multicriterion models effective for one type of decision frequently occurring in industry.

Consider a large number of alternatives and a large number of criteria, where "large" means greater than four and less than, say, five hundred. Suppose that each criterion ranks the alternatives according to its weak ordering, from the best to the worst one. Our decision problem consists of ranking the alternatives from the best to the worst according to a nontrivial weak ordering that is a legitimate synthesis of the criteria. We call this problem the industrial outranking problem.

Since the publication of Arrow's impossibility theorem [1951] and Black's work, summarized in his book [1958], much effort has been spent on the analysis and rationalization of committee decision-making. Noncontroversial progress in the theory of social choice and in committee decision techniques has come from the study of strategic voting (see, for instance, Gibbard [1973] and Satterthwaite [1975]) and from what has been called implementation (see, for instance, Fine and Fine [1974]). There has been less consensus in the field of multicriterion operations research. The accent has been on building a large collection of multicriterion decision-making recipes without being able to decide which of them were the best. Papers like "Douze méthodes d'analyse multicritère" (Twelve methods for multicriterion decision-making), by G. Bernard and M. L. Besson [1971], show great ingenuity in inventing new recipes. It is difficult, however, to determine which one makes more sense than the others.

A celebrated example of such a recipe is the Electre Method in its early development (cf. Susmann et al. [1967] or, for a short presentation, annex 1). For over ten years, at least in France, many discerning managers have thought that Electre was *the* way to deal with difficult multicriterion decision-making, even though this method, as far as we know, does not satisfy any system of consistent and appealing axioms.

We think that the professional decision maker should know that, especially in multicriterion analysis, he can be the victim of a series of personal biases that he should wish to avoid. In particular, he should hope for something better than just a recipe—rather, a true method that would at least appear to have solid foundations. Through dealing with **real** problems, it is clear that a recipe that allows for creativity, intuition, and adaptation to specific conditions will perform better than any elegant mathematical model. But if the recipe is inspired by safe principles, the decision maker should avoid the danger of using a method either so versatile that it will not prevent the influence of his personal biases or so artificially rigid that its application would appear unacceptable.

A few indisputable lessons arise nevertheless from the success of the Electre Method:

1. Decision makers liked the way Electre somehow describes an ideal behavior, extending to a large number of

criteria and alternatives a technique not without psycho-logical value for small sets of data.

2. Decision makers enjoyed very much being able to understand the principles of the method.

3. With its large collection of arbitrary parameters, Electre is a very versatile method, which did not diminish the responsibility of the decision maker in the decision process.

These three points stress qualities that any effective method should possess.

The motivations that have inspired our work on the in-dustrial outranking problem are simple:

• On one hand, ranking into a reasonable number of classes finite sets of "projects" already ordered according to a finite number of (most of the time) qualitative criteria became, for one of us, a daily burden! He felt that he had to offer more than a list of empirical recipes. In addition, he shared the assertion made by Eckenrode [1965] and pointed out by Johnsen [1968] that the more ordinal the data, the more consistent the result.

• On the other hand, the work on social choice was almost the only theoretical approach dealing with the foundations of multicriterion decision-making, in the domain where the decision consists in ordering a finite set of alternatives already ranked according to a finite set of criteria.

These two reasons explain our conscious limitation to the purely ordinal case and our research technique; it is by extending and translating present results in social choice theory that we found the main results presented in this book.

The first one is an extended list of conditions for efficacy of the majority method when applied to our case, not alge-braic conditions but conditions with interpretations satis-factory for an industrial problem. The second result shows that these cases of applicability of the majority method form, statistically speaking, an asymptotically null set; in other words, these conditions will be met in practice only in very exceptional cases. The third result is a noncontradictory axiomatic system that makes sense for the industrial outranking problem (a system that includes a generalization of the Condorcet condition). And the fourth result is the identification of some of the practical methods satisfying this axiomatic system and the study of some of their properties.

All these concerns have induced the following outline of the book. Its first part is devoted to some of the simplest classical psychological considerations and results, which, further on, will help us to model an ordering process that allows for conflicting and incommensurable criteria. The fact that the more satisfactory axiomatic systems lead directly to unacceptable paradoxes will be treated in this first part. Because of its huge historical importance, the majority method, along with its limitations and its domain of efficacy, will comprise the entire second part. It will be shown how indeed it is theoretically of limited interest in solving our industrial decision maker's problem. The third and last part will concentrate on the new axiomatic system, which leads to practical techniques solving satisfactorily this same problem.

The research and writing of this book was carried out at the Center for Research on Organizational Efficiency, at the Institute for Mathematical Studies in the Social Sciences at Stanford University, under contract ONR-N00014-79-C-0685 with the United States Office of Naval Research. We are grateful to all these agencies for their support.

Part I

1   The Problem

This chapter contains a miscellany that indeed could be omitted from our subject, being devoted to purely mathematical questions. But it seemed appropriate to outline the type of multicriterion ranking process that suggested the logical itinerary followed throughout the book. The problem is precisely one met everyday by one of us, as a consultant in industrial decision-making.

When hired to consult, it is very often about an ordering process in which two steps can be clearly identified:

1. an identification step, which consists of selecting relevant alternatives and selecting relevant criteria—both very approximate operations;

2. a processing step, which consists of selecting an aggregation method (selection is usually reduced to the mere acceptance of the first method proposed) and applying it to the data, and almost in any case a weighted majority method.

It is through the description of these steps that the needs of the decision scientist we hope to fulfill in this book will be made obvious.

1.1 The Identification Step

1.1.1 Selecting Relevant Alternatives Is an Approximate Operation

When a decision maker has to make one of the **decisions** we have in mind, he identifies a set of alternatives as being the supposedly competing ones. This set can seem very restricted (e.g., selection of one best candidate among a few or choice of a best strategy among a small number of proposals). More often, its limits are not so clearly fixed; one can have to take into account last minute candidates, or new combinations of strategies suggested by last minute information.

A small number of alternatives is the exception; a large but finite set of possibilities is the rule. This extensive set of alternatives is often represented by a continuum. Our methodology is to take the alternatives as identified by the decision maker (i.e., a large but finite set); but we attempt to derive methods that avoid the risk of instability in the results caused by the introduction or the deletion of a really noncompeting alternative. In other words, in those methods, only an outstanding new alternative would be able to disturb the ranking of the best elements.

1.1.2 Selecting Criteria Is Very Approximate As Well

Our decision maker also identifies a set of criteria that are supposed to be the pertinent ones for the decision.

We distinguish between two types of criteria:

a. *attributes,* which are rather well identified aspects of the alternatives, but are only correlated with the desired outcome of the alternatives;

b. *objectives,* which are directly connected with the desired outcomes, but for which the estimation will be in general fuzzy.

Consider, as an example, the choice of advanced research projects for new production in a business firm. Let the desired outcome be a very profitable project. Correlated with this outcome, "having a fast return on investment" can be the first financial objective. The statement, "The head of the research lab thinks that the project is the most feasible from among the others," is only an attribute. But because its evaluation will be much more accurate than the evaluation of the financial objective, it will likely be more important.

In industrial multicriterion problems, we mainly encounter multiattribute problems. In this sense, the expected profit of an alternative can generally be considered as an attribute, when the desired outcome will, for instance, be to make safer the equilibrium of the productions of the firm. These attributes, easily obtained from the decision makers, are likely to be very large in number. For instance, Duncker [1903] already quotes attributes related to

- market standing,
- innovation level,
- productivity,
- physical and financial resources,
- profitability,
- manager performance and development,
- public responsibility.

In the M.A.R.S.A.N. method (Susmann et al. [1967]), as many as 49 potentially valid attributes were listed and actually taken into account.

In developing a recent model for the selection of

diversification projects in an international business firm, a committee of the top decision makers in the firm suggested to one of us for their particular case not less than 25 strongly independent criteria.

1.2 The Aggregation Process

Underlying the criteria are ordinal preference structures: in other words, criteria that may look a priori to be numerical in nature can often be expressed as semiorders without any loss of information. Let us, for instance, consider the size of the investment required by a project. For many firms, it is not the numerical value of the investment that is important but the fact that the firm is used to dealing with this "precise" size of investment. From five to seven equivalence classes will in general be sufficient to describe the size of the investment precisely.

The name of aggregation is due to the fact that the desired result of the process is similarly a semiorder, with a reasonable number of equivalence classes. The frequency of this problem in industry is easy to understand. Let us consider a set of projects for a particular business firm. The real decision will be to realize some of these projects. During the course of their realization, some should rapidly prove unfeasible, some will need to be deleted, some, on the contrary, will suddenly become obsolete. The effective realization of an industrial project is highly unpredictable, and the best tool for a decision maker is a priority order on the projects, judged independently, in such a way that if a project has to be abandoned, or if the available budget for the projects is enlarged, the new projects to be realized will be the next ones along the "aggregated" order.

1.2.1   Then Comes the Choice of an Aggregation Method

What really happens inside a man's brain when he undertakes such a complex operation as in a multicriterion aggregation is still a conjecture. Even for very simple decisions indeed, we are far from being able to present realistic models of the phenomenon. As a proof of this assertion, we need only recall the experiments of Ungar [1973] on darkness avoidance in the rat. Conditioning rats to make the decision—from a learning process—to avoid darkness and prefer light leads to the synthesis, by the brain of the animal, of a special polypeptide, called scoptophobin, the presence of which in the brain is significantly correlated with darkness avoidance in nonconditioned rats. The building of such a substance is the result of an extremely complex mechanism, which we cannot even imagine. We are hence condemned to make a phenomenological model of what happens in the brain by only looking at very superficial, but indisputable, facts.

For instance, we know that a decision maker tries to make his decisions through knowledge and enlightening experiences. For an important decision, he would like to be able to process all the information his memory has stored that would be relevant to the subject. This, of course, cannot be done, and this impossibility can be explained especially by the structure of memory. For one hundred years (Ebbinghaus [1885]), it has been known that a human brain possesses a short-term memory that allows the storage, for a very limited time, of a very limited number of items available for treatment. Even if training this memory can prove effective in the increase of the performance, its capacity remains quite limited (as everyday experience confirms).

A human long-term memory, on the contrary, stores so many items in a lifetime that its huge capacity can be considered unlimited. However, if these data have to be retrieved for treatment, it will be through a linear chain of associations, and the process for retrieval will be relatively long and somewhat painful: try, for instance, to remember a birthday once forgotten! The same process is, when unconscious, considered by some authors as describing intuition, which can seem much more efficient. But intuition is well known for not being guaranteed, and one should feel it inappropriate to leave the responsibility of a dangerous decision to a process totally uncontrolled and subject to many errors and biases.

We have to admit that a regular brain is not built in order to make complex multicriterion decisions: the quantity of information is too large to allow a simultaneous treatment by the short-term memory, and there is no clearly dominant methodology allowing a progressive treatment. This is often typical of the urge for help expressed by many decision makers: they estimate that they are not able to consider concurrently all the projects and all the desirable criteria in order to make the decision as they would like.

They have often, however, the feeling, and sometimes enough intuition, to make the decision effectively from a small number of criteria applied to a small number of alternatives. Based on personal experience, we estimate four criteria and as many alternatives to be the maximum humanly tractable complexity.

The task of the scientist who wishes to help the decision maker should be relatively easy, as long as the latter will be able to explain clearly his way of processing a small amount of data: it can be conjectured that his inability to solve bigger problems comes in large proportion from the limitations of the short-term memory.

The decision maker is almost never able to suggest a set of noncontradictory axioms, which would be the set he actually uses; rather he expresses the axioms he would like to follow; as we shall see in the next chapter, the more appealing the hypotheses, the more infeasible appears the corresponding axiomatic system.

1.2.2   The Weighted Majority Deadlock

Strangely, one part of the recipe, which is rather wishful thinking, is popular among the decision makers, and deserves to be described. Very often, after the evaluation of the alternatives for all the criteria, the decision maker realizes that his problem is not made easier. A little disappointed, he expresses the feeling that the light will come from "weighting" the criteria. The decision maker implicitly then builds up the following dangerous model. He considers a committee in which the criterion i is associated with W_i members of identical behavior, W_i being the integer weight of the criterion i. He will then apply the majority method of decision.

We think that these committee members, in order to make the model realistic, should not behave like committee members. For instance, they should not act strategically (a technical criterion of not being shrewd). In spite of this, the decision models that are then used by the decision makers are identical to the procedures used in committee decision-making: they begin by trying the weighted majority method. For reasons that will be made clear, it almost never works. Then they have to use methods, such as Borda's very widespread method, that have been thought of only for the case of committee decisions and appear inappropriate. Through this process, they obtain for diverse reasons, results that, even if appropriate to committees, usually do not conveniently solve industrial multicriterion decision-making. As a consequence, faced with the lack of a convenient method, the decision maker prefers to wait until the last moment to make the ranking decision. This attitude allows him to benefit, more or less consciously, either from additional information that will legitimately influence the choice and will make it easier or from a state of emergency imposing one survival criterion over the others. This attitude, of course, does not solve the question, but we tend to believe that the "weighting" of the pros and cons yields some insight.

Weighting can be considered as a direct measure of the reinforcement of a learning process: a criterion that has often been correlated in the past with success or failure will naturally be granted a higher "weight." We know of no experimentation supporting the fact, but it fits with Ungar's experiments: a special polypeptide is present in the brain of rats submitted to a special training, and this polypeptide acts as a facilitator to the learning of this behavior when injected into untrained rats, as additional weights for the corresponding criteria.

One must add (which is confirmed by our experience) that the weights given by the decision maker are always subject to considerable fluctuations from one day to the next, even from one hour to the next! But the fact that they insist on assigning weights probably means that any serious method will have to cope with unstable weights. In other words, the method should not be too sensitive to a change in the weights. Practical experience shows (which was anyway very likely) that a very restricted set of permitted weights is often enough to satisfy the urge for precision expressed by the decision maker.

In conclusion, we have to recognize that, in industrial problems, *many criteria with inconstant weights and many alternatives in a domain with variable frontiers* will constitute the data from which a decision has to be made. The decision maker would then need methods ranking the alternatives from the best to the worst, in order to choose the best ones inside a limited budget. Many books on industrial decision-making, which do not dare to fight on dangerous battlefields, insists on the analysis of the set of alternatives, and on their ranking along the criteria, without mention of any aggregation method. They claim that a good solution will emerge naturally from a good analysis.

On the contrary, we think that the decision maker does not need the intervention of a decision scientist in the cases where the solution emerges so easily, and the content of this book tends to show that the choice of an effective aggregation model has to be closely dependent on the context. By this we mean the nature of the data as well as the external context of the decision.

This book will help, we hope, the decision scientist to make clearer the domain of application of the just quoted weighted majority method, and will propose, in order to fight the weaknesses of this method, a set of methods with axiomatic justification taking into account the special outline of industrial choices.

2 The Paradoxes

There is very likely no unique method used by minds to make decisions. It is well known that individuals are generally not very logical, and that their decision behavior can be modified by the surrounding culture or by the acquisition of some special skill. In spite of this, it has to be admitted that, given a specific decision, a specific mind will use a specific method.

The decision process will then fail if the data are too heavy for the brain capacities of treatment, if the method is inadequate, or if the problem has no real solution (which can mean that the set of alternatives has been overrestricted).

We explained previously that the aim of models in operations research should be only to improve upon—as it becomes necessary—the natural, but then unsuccessful, method of a real decision maker. Very often, however, unable to explain what his brain does or should do, the decision maker, when interviewed about his multicriterion decision process, will answer by describing a set of axioms that he tries to follow. Of course, it would be ideal if the mathematician had only to listen to a set of axioms, and could derive from them a list of consistent corresponding methods. But the straightforward application of this process works much more poorly than one would like. In what follows, we shall even show how the two more natural ways to do it lead to a complete—or at least very substantial—failure.

Remember that our scope is limited, in terms of decision-making problems, to the cases where criteria and alternatives are finite in number. Each criterion consists of a linear ranking of the alternatives. We denote by X the set of alternatives, by $\Omega = (\theta_1, \ldots, \theta_N)$ the indexed set of criteria, by $E(X)$ a profile $\{\theta_1(X), \ldots, \theta_N(X)\}$. For any Y included in X, $E(Y)$ will denote the sequence $\theta_1(Y), \ldots, \theta_N(Y)$ of the restrictions of the θ_i to only the elements in Y.

2.1 Arrow's Axiomatic System

Since a full-scale discussion of Arrow's theorem is not within the scope of this book, we shall use a restricted but very simple form of the result: the criteria are taken to be total rankings of the alternatives. Additionally, the set of criteria and the set of alternatives are both finite and each contains more than two elements. We suppose that we need a method D able to give, for each profile, one satisfying total ranking of the alternatives deserving the name of multicriterion ranking. We shall call D a multicriterion decision function.

Axiom 2.1 (Unrestricted domain)
The criteria should be unrestricted and D should respect unanimity. Hence, the values that can be taken by the criteria and the decision function will be unrestricted.

Axiom 2.2 (Independence of irrelevant alternatives)
If D denotes the multicriterion decision function, X denotes the set of alternatives, and $\theta_1, \ldots, \theta_N$ the sequence of criteria, then $\forall Y \subset X, D[E(X)](Y) = D(E(Y))$.

In other words, the restriction of the multicriterion ranking to only the alternatives in Y is the result one obtains by applying the method to the restriction of the criteria to only the alternatives in Y.

This means that it is of no importance for the decision if you have forgotten in the application of the method some (poorly ranked) alternatives: we know from our first chapter that the complete set of alternatives is always very large and only a relatively small subset can be identified. It is thus essential that the result of the method on a small set of alternatives not vary if forgotten alternatives are taken into consideration.

Axiom 2.3 (Positive responsiveness)
Let us consider a pair of alternatives $\{x,y\}$ such that $D[E(X)]$ restricted to $\{x,y\}$ ranks x before y.

Let A be the set of the criteria that ranked x before y in E.

If E' is another profile where the criteria in A still rank x before y, then the restriction of $D[E'(X)]$ to $\{x,y\}$ should still rank x before y.

The axiom, written in this form, contains, of course, axiom 2.2, but in terms of interpretation, it is interesting to separate axiom 2.3, which only means, in a weak but precise form, that the more the criteria judge that some alternative should outrank some other, the more likely it is to be found in the value of the decision.

Let us now consider two alternatives, say, x, y, in this order and a set G_D^{xy} of criteria such that if the criteria in G_D^{xy}, for a particular profile E, unanimously rank x before y, then $(D(E))(\{x,y\}) = (x,y)$.

In other words, G_D^{xy} is a set of criteria such that, when applying D, their unanimity in ranking x before y assures the fact that x will be before y in the multicriterion decision ranking.

Any such set will be said to be decisive for $\{x,y\}$. Such sets always exist (e.g., the unanimity of criteria is a decisive set for any pair $\{x,y\}$ according to axiom 2.1). What is more, they can be uniquely characterized as follows:

Consider any profile $E(X)$ such that, in $D[E(X)]$, x is before y. The set of criteria that placed x before y in $E(X)$ is a decisive set for $\{x,y\}$. This is a direct application of axiom 2.3.

We can now proceed with the proof of Arrow's result.

Lemma 2.1
Any G_D^{xy} such that $|G_D^{xy}| \geqslant 2$ contains one smaller decisive set.

Proof Consider a profile E where the criteria in G_D^{xy} are separated into two nonempty sets G' and G''. Then consider a third alternative z and restrict the profile E to the set $\{x,y,z\}$. Denote the complement of a set S by $\mathbf{C}S$. Suppose G' ranks the alternatives z,x,y; G'' ranks the alternatives x,y,z; and, $\mathbf{C}G_D^{xy}$ ranks the alternatives y,z,x. In $D(E\{x,y,z\}))$, x will necessarily be before y, but z can occupy any of the three remaining ranks. However:

1. If $D(E(\{x,y,z\})) = (z,x,y)$, then, as the criteria in G' are the only ones that rank z before y, G' is G_D^{zy}.
2. If $D(E(\{x,y,z\})) = (x,y,z)$, then, as the criteria in G'' are the only ones that rank x before z, G'' is G_D^{xz}.
3. If $D(E(\{x,y,z\})) = (x,z,y)$, then, for the same reasons as in (1) and (2), G' is G_D^{zy} and G'' is G_D^{xz}.

Lemma 2.2
Any G_D^{xy} is G_D^{wz} for any (w,z).

Proof Consider E_1, in which all the criteria in G (which is G_D^{xy}) rank w before x before y and those in $\mathbf{C}G$ rank y before

w before x. $D(E_1)$ places x before y, as G ranked x before y, and w before x by unanimity (axiom 2.1).

Then $D(E_1) = (w,x,y)$, which contains w before y. As only the criteria in G ranked w before y, G is G_D^{wy}.

Consider E_2 in which all the criteria in G (which is now G_D^{wy}) rank w before y before z when those in CG rank y before z before w. For similar reasons, G is G_D^{wz}. The conclusion now, of course, follows immediately.

From lemma 2.1 applied recursively, there is a decisive set of one criterion, and from lemma 2.2, it is decisive on any pair of alternatives, hence on any ranking. In other words, the decision function is identical to the ranking of this unique criterion.

Theorem 2.1
A multicriterion decision function satisfying axioms 2.1, 2.2, and 2.3 must coincide with exactly one of the criteria.

You wanted to make a real, wise, *multi*criterion decision, and the simplest and most natural axioms drive you toward a *mono*criterion one!

In the political sciences, Arrow's axiomatic system is considered to be necessary for a democracy (in which voters are the criteria), and the paradox is that it leads to dictatorship.

In our context, this result suggests that one particular criterion should overcome the influence of the others. Maybe, if the set of criteria has the good luck to contain one that efficiently combines the others, from among the possible "dictatorships" at least one will be acceptable.

What does all of this mean in practice? Let us look at what probably works and what probably does not in a real, then in an ideal, decision maker's brain.

As we discussed earlier, a human decision maker probably uses different methods at different stages. Some elimination steps are probably undertaken in order to verify that all characteristics of the alternatives meet certain minimal requirements. The remaining ones will be admissible candidates.

The mind will then proceed to rank the candidates by means of more or less conscious methods. For biological reasons, we suppose that no method involving sophisticated global calculations can be used by the brain. As a consequence, a "dictatorship" of one utility criterion will occur in a brain only if this utility is available with almost no calculation.

We have in effect supposed earlier that in the type of decision problems which we solve here, the time needed to construct a valid numerical model for the trade-off ratios would in any case be considerable enough to ensure their obsolescence before use.

If "weights" have been so popular in the multicriterion literature, it is because something like weighting probably occurs often. This "something" can be described either as the approximate computation of a linear function or, in less numerical issues, as the aggregation of pairwise comparisons, obtained from the weighting of a not very constant battery of criteria. In fact, as soon as the brain cannot easily find a unique criterion that clearly synthesizes the others, it will decide to separate the analysis along different criteria (related to different past situations which can introduce many irrelevant items) and will begin to falter.

Why should it be so fuzzy?

1. Because the brain is not able to concentrate its attention on a large number of items that are themselves ranked by a large number of criteria.

2. Because the brain is probably not able to rank with precision all possible alternatives along all possible criteria.

3. Because during the ranking of a long series of alternatives, the set of relevant criteria can be substantially altered: for instance, if the first fifty alternatives have all called for a certain set of criteria and a new criterion becomes pertinent from the fifty-first alternative onward, the brain might well stick to the criteria that have been "efficient" for fifty! And this only because of functional fixity (Duncker [1903]).

It is thus on a very uncertain background that the brain has to build a method of decision. Remember that it cannot do much, because its most sophisticated capabilities of treatment are limited to a local, very small area of memory. This can explain the success of certain "simple" minds that stick to one idea, to one criterion, and can, by this means, always decide in the same coherent direction. This is, of course, rarely the best solution, and it is in fact the multitude of counterexamples that drove operational researchers away from, for example, a maximized profit that would not be balanced by the risk of generating strikes!

2.2 May's Axiomatic System

As a counterpoint to dictatorship, public opinion has, since the Marquis de Condorcet [1785], considered the simple majority rule as a panacea. In this method alternative a will be ranked before alternative b in the decision if and only if a majority of criteria ranks a before b.

Although this method was universally adopted, it was not until 1952 that it became characterized by an axiomatic system making sense from the decision point of view. The detailed discussion of this axiomatic system will be found in May [1952]. Let us recall it here briefly.

The set of possible decisions is limited to two alternatives, x and y. The individuals can vote $+1$ (which means x

before y), -1, or 0 (which means indifference). The decision can be $+1$, -1, or 0.

The proper axioms are

1. The decision rule is well and everywhere defined.

2. The decision rule is symmetric (i.e., neutral with respect to the individuals as well as the alternatives). This condition can be expressed by two subconditions: (a) the decision depends only on the number of votes for $+1$, -1, and 0; and (b) if $f(d_1, \ldots, d_N)$ denotes the value of the decision when the voter i votes d_i, then $f(-d_1, \ldots, -d_N) = -f(d_1, \ldots, d_N)$.

3. The decision has the property of positive responsiveness: if $f(d_1, \ldots, d_N) \geq 0$, for all i, $d_i' \geq d_i$, and for at least one i_0, $d_{i_0}' > d_{i_0}$, then $f(d_1', \ldots, d_N') = 1$.

The fundamental consequence of these axioms is the following.

Theorem 2.2
The decision rule that satisfies May's axiomatic system is unique: it is the simple majority decision rule.

Proof Let us define a profile as an indexed set of individual ballots corresponding to a simple issue. Consider any profile $(d_1, \ldots, d_N)$ where the number of those who voted $+1$ equals the number of those who voted -1:

$$f(d_1, \ldots, d_N) = f(-d_1, \ldots, -d_N) = -f(d_1, \ldots, d_N) = 0.$$

Any additional ballot in favor of $+1$ would shift (cf. axiom 2.3) the decision f to the state $+1$.

Considering the symmetric profile, it is clear that any additional vote in favor of -1 would push the decision to the state -1, and thus the theorem is proved.

So, up to this point, the majority method has the nice outlook we would like for our aggregation method. This could by itself be a sufficient reason to explain the huge success of the majority method. This success can be equally credited to the excellent opportunities for strategies that the method offers to the shrewd.

2.3 Strategic Majority Voting

The previous part shows that if a vote is taken once and if only two alternatives are compared, the majority method works in a satisfactory way. Grave problems occur for a succession of votes and for more than two alternatives.

2.3.1 The Cake

Let us consider, for instance, a cake to be shared among 100 people. Suppose one of them has some power and political training. His first aim will be to grant undue favors to, say, 50 people against the other 49. With their "cooperation" thus ensured he will form the "Party of the 51." These 51 are going to use majority voting to decide legally to throw 49 people in jail and redistribute their 49 shares among the 51 members of the party.

This shrewd person, if not overcome by a competitor, will again make alliances to form a new Party of the 26, etc., until only two people remain as potential cake-eaters! The majority method has concentrated power and goods into the hands of a few.

2.3.2 The Drunkard, the Miser, and the Health Freak

The majority method can work much more discreetly to the same effect, if the members of an assembly use strategic amendment techniques.

The theorems that can be obtained say roughly that if your assembly is divided enough, if there are enough alternatives, and if you master the formulation of amendments and the order in which they will be voted upon, you can reach any arbitrary final outcome.

A very well known example has been given by Farquharson [1969]. A drunkard, a miser, and a health freak are the three members of a committee that must decide how to spend the money of a foundation. When dying, the witty millionaire who gave the money insisted on building a student residence on Stanford's campus at the proper time.

For the miser, now is too early: the money would be better used accruing interest slowly in a bank.

For the health freak, now is the proper time; a very salubrious house should be built, naturally without a bar.

Of course for the drunkard, now may be the proper time, but what kind of house would not have a bar!?

Three alternatives are hence determined:

1. no house;

2. house without a bar;

3. house with a bar;

and the natural rankings of the three men are

Miser: 1,2,3;

Health freak: 2,1,3;

Drunkard: 3,1,2.

The majority method applies, and gives 1,2,3; 1 is said to be the Condorcet winner. But if the health freak were president, he would suggest voting on "... the only important question after all: shall we build the house *now*, or put the money in a bank and *wait*?"

The decision to build now would pass by a two-thirds majority.

Satisfied with the result of this first vote, the health freak would next introduce the question of the bar; the bar would be rejected by another two-thirds majority.

The final result is a house without a bar.

It seems to the authors of this book that the unconscious mind can work as did the health freak, to eliminate alternatives sequentially. In large scale problems, because the short-term memory is small, the local treatment of the alternatives may very well eliminate a Condorcet winner, and even lead to an obnoxious choice (as above!).

More generally, one can wonder whether strategic considerations should be introduced in the analysis of industrial processes: the criteria will be in general evaluated by official experts inside the firm, and their judgments have no reason to avoid conscious or unconscious biases.

At first glance, one would think that a method prohibiting manipulations would probably be more efficient. But Gibbard [1973] and Satterthwaite [1975] proved that only the dictatorship of one criterion over the others could provide this nonmanipulability. Other researchers, such as Peleg [1978] and Dutta and Pattanaik [1978], tried to characterize voting processes where an equal shrewdness of the experts would lead to results similar to those obtained in case of optimal objectivity. But even in this case, we are still far from reality where shrewdness is unevenly spread.

But this is not the most serious objection to the use of the majority method in the brain of an ideal decision maker.

Let $\{a,b,c\}$ be a set of three alternatives. Let us suppose that only three criteria are considered, with roughly equal weighting:

if the first criterion indicates a before b before c,

if the second criterion indicates b before c before a,

if the third criterion indicates c before a before b,

the application of the majority method will indicate that a is preferred to b, b is preferred to c, but c is itself preferred to a.

The mind in which this happens can take the alternatives in turn without finding a most preferred alternative.

This is the celebrated "voting paradox," pointed out by M. J. A. M. C. Marquis de Condorcet [1785]. The paradox, if rarely observed, would remain a purely theoretical problem. This is not at all the case.

Shortly, we shall see that the stochastic model of individual votes that are evenly distributed among the set of orderings on X gives, if both the number of alternatives and the number of criteria increase without limit, a probability for the voting paradox that tends rapidly toward one.

G. Th. Guilbaud [1968] gave a .088 limit for this probability when the number of alternatives is fixed at three while only the number of criteria increases. More recent computational work on the subject can be found in Fishburn, Gehrlein, and Maskin [1979].

It arises from this last work that in decisions with many criteria and alternatives, the Condorcet effect will occur extremely frequently. This troublesome difficulty has an importance that can be measured by the multitude of papers that have been devoted to the calculation of the related probabilities. It is very strange to observe, in contrast, the small number of equivalent computations completed for other multicriterion decision methods. This probably shows that in multicriterion problems the mind will always try first to apply the majority method.

Black [1948], Coombs [1954], and Arrow [1951], then Romero [1978] (only quoting the extremities of the chain) suggested conditions based on human sciences that would imply the transitivity of majority voters. These will be discussed in part II.

Part II

Introduction to Part II

Throughout the second part we shall discuss two topics: an extensive collection of conditions that, although very restrictive, model particular cases and ensure the efficacy of the majority method; and a very strong and restrictive limit on the overall applicability of the majority method to the general problem.

We shall use the following notation:

- X denotes a finite set $\{a,b, \ldots ,z\}$ of objects called alternatives.

- E (or $E(X)$) denotes a profile, i.e., a sequence of N rankings (in other words, total orders, permutations, linear orderings) $\theta_1, \theta_2, \ldots, \theta_N$ of the $n = |X|$ considered alternatives. Each θ_i will be called a criterion.

- $\forall Y \subset X$, $\theta_i(Y)$ will denote the restrictions of $\theta_i(X)$ to only the alternatives in Y.

- If $Y \subset X$, $E(Y)$ denotes the sequence given by the restrictions of the θ_i to only the alternatives in Y.

- The description "the last rank in $E(Y)$" will mean the last rank in all the $\theta_i(Y)$.

We maintain it is not pertinent to our theoretical background to examine cases involving ties. One can in effect temporarily suppose that if it were necessary, any criterion could be refined enough to make the ties on the criterion disappear; the objects will therefore always be ranked in different ranks according to each criterion.

Another distinction we find irrelevant is counting on an odd or an even number of individual votes, since adding or deleting a criterion is always possible in a real multicriterion decision.

Although we are actually considering a majority method with weighted criteria, we can always suppose that the weights are integers and that their determination is exterior to the real problematic procedure of deciding. Doing this turns all of the "weighted majority" problems described into "simple majority" problems with equal weights for all criteria.

Part II is itself divided into four chapters. Chapter 3 deals with the restricted domains having a known socioeconomic interpretation. Chapter 4 builds the algebraic framework underlying these conditions, and Chapter 5 repairs a classical error on another set of celebrated conditons. Chapter 6 indicates how drastically restrictive are even the loosest of these conditions in terms of structural requirements on the criteria and draws from this operational concluding remarks on the use of the majority method for real noncommittee multicriteria decision-making.

3

A First Set of Conditions for the Transitivity of Majority Rule

The conditons described henceforth almost always require an odd number of criteria. As we discussed earlier, this requirement is of no importance for the applications that we are considering; we shall always assume an odd number of criteria. Likewise, the number of alternatives will always be assumed at least three—since the case of two alternatives in the majority method has been investigated previously.

The conditions described in this chapter are all particular cases of the final one. For this reason the proof of their efficacy to ensure the transitivity of the majority method of decision will be given with this last case.

For each condition its interest for applications will be discussed. We shall describe

1. Coombs's condition,
2. Black's condition (unimodality),
3. Romero's arboricity,
4. Romero's quasi-unimodality,
5. Arrow's and Black's single-peakedness.

3.1 Coombs's Condition

Coombs [1954] pointed out that some very dominant cultural features, coupled with the lack of urge for strategic voting (as can happen inside a mind), could explain the statistically surprising efficacy of the majority method. This was especially true for committee decision-making.

Let π be a numerical function on X that assigns to each alternative x a number $\pi(x)$. Let the criterion i be obtained from, say, an ideal number Π_i: the best object for criterion i, x_i^1, will minimize $|\pi(x) - \Pi_i|$ over X, the second best will minimize the same function over $X - \{x_i^1\}$, and so on. A profile where all the criteria are obtained through such a process, with a common π and a set of Π_i corresponding to the different criteria, is said to follow Coombs's condition.

It will be made clearer in the following example: let us consider a committee in charge of some budget, whose immediate task is to rank a set of proposals for a given project. Suppose that the common culture of the committee members strongly emphasizes money and that the cost of each proposal is well known. We can say that proposals are ranked along a common numerical reference axis.

One can imagine that each member has in mind not an ideal proposal, but an ideal amount to spend on this project. Then, if individual i has the ideal budget B_i in mind, he will rank proposal x before proposal y if and only if the absolute value of the difference between B_i and the budget of x is smaller than the absolute value of the difference between B_i and the budget of y.

Suppose now that, believing in democracy, they vote according to their feelings. The resulting profile will be said to follow Coombs's condition and the majority method will then give a transitive result. This comes from the following simple property shared by all the methods in this chapter.

Lemma 3.1

If three alternatives, say, x,y,z, are ordered xyz along a common numerical reference axis, and the voters follow Coombs's condition, then for any individual ranking θ,

$\theta(\{x,y,x\})$ cannot be x,z,y or z,x,y.

In other words, from $\{x,y,z\}$, y cannot be ranked last.

The proof is very simple. Let m_{xy}, m_{yz}, and m_{xz} be the respective midpoints of the segments xy, yz, and xz. When an ideal point comes from the left, the corresponding ranking is xyz. Then it crosses over m_{xy}, and the ranking becomes yxz. Then it crosses m_{xz}; the ranking becomes yzx. Then m_{yz}, and the ranking becomes and stays zyx. In conclusion, y is never the last.

We shall show below that this proposition ensures the transitivity of the majority method of decision.

One very important point, of course, is to find out how restrictive this condition is in terms of, for instance, restrictions on the individual freedom of the voters.

Coombs's opinion was that culture was very often responsible for a spontaneous realization of this condition: under the reference data, the numerical structure that we have described would be tacitly present.

In terms of operational multicriterion decision-making, one does not see why a criterion should follow such a culture constraint, and one cannot speak of individual freedom.

In Coombs's case, as long as the individual can freely choose his optimal budget and vote according to his conviction, one cannot speak of a limitation of the individual freedom; more precisely, there is no feeling of limitation of freedom even under strong cultural biases. In the second case, on the contrary, it is clear that the number of possible rankings allowed to a criterion is limited. Let us now denote $|X| = n$.

Definition 3.1 (Degree of variety)
Let C be a condition of transitivity for the majority method. We call *degree of variety allowed by* C the ratio, denoted $f(n)$ = $F(n)/n!$, where $F(n)$ is the maximum number of different rankings that can be observed as values taken by the criteria in a profile following condition C (hence $n!$ is the number of total rankings on X). This measure of the restriction is thus inherent to the condition and independent of any cultural biases.

An important remark has to be made about this definition: if the function π could be chosen a posteriori, any total order would give a possible ranking for a criterion. The distinction between the potential values that can be taken by an isolated criterion and the same values inside an actual experimental context has to be stressed. The degree of variety is an a posteriori measure. We consider an actual profile E following a condition of transitivity of the majority method such that any additional criterion with a ranking of the alternatives different from the rankings in E would break the condition. The largest number of criteria in E is $F(n)$.

Theorem 3.1
For Coombs's condition

$$F(n) = \frac{n(n-1)}{2} + 1.$$

Proof Consider a given situation and rank the alternatives along the common numerical reference axis, at their corresponding abscissa. When the ideal point of a voter goes from the left to the right, the corresponding vote changes. It changes at each point that is midway between two alternatives. There are $n(n-1)/2$ such points. The result is then trivial.

Numerically speaking:

n	3	6	10	20
$f(n)$	.667	.022	$(1.27)10^{-5}$	$\sim 10^{-16}$

3.2 Black's Condition

A straightforward generalization of this condition was given by Black [1948, 1958].

His condition is quite similar to Coombs's, but Black's common cultural reference is limited to a mere ranking. This can be described by diverse equivalent formulations.

Intuitively speaking, one can, for instance, consider the alternatives as being ranked along a thread made of rubber. Each voter could unevenly stretch the thread as desired and would then cast his ballot according to Coombs's technique.

Another way is to describe an algorithm for the individual rankings. Considering the common reference ordering R, the individual i will rank any object as the preferred object. If the distance between the two objects is, for instance, equal to the number of ranks that separates them in R, the object ranked second by individual i will be one of the two nearest objects along the reference ordering R (or the nearest if it is unique). The object ranked third will be one of the two remaining nearest (or the second nearest if it is unique) from among the not already chosen, and so on.

It is clear that if the three alternatives x,y,z are ordered in this way in R, the individuals will never rank y in the third position among the three objects of the triple. It is clear also, from the algorithm, that the last object in an individual ranking must be one of the two extremes in R. Then, if the last-ranked object is determined, and is, say, z, the second-to-last object must necessarily be one of the two extremes in $R[X - z]$, and so on.

This is, of course, another algorithmic formulation of the condition: the individual can determine his ballot through a progressive ranking of the remaining extreme alternatives in R.

Theorem 3.2
For Black's condition, $F(n) = 2^{n-1}$.

Proof Trivial, from this last algorithm. Numerically speaking this condition offers a much less restrictive structure than Coombs's condition.

		4	5	6	7
$f(n)$	Coombs	7/24	11/120	.022	.004
	Black	8/24	16/120	.044	.012

Black's condition has often been called unimodality for the following reason: if you plot the possible individual utilities of the alternatives for a particular voter along the reference order, their shape will show a unique mode.

David Romero [1978] gave a very nice algorithm (linear in time with respect to n) pointing out any and all possible reference orders for which a given profile would satisfy Black's condition. Its description can be found in annex 2.

Romero described in his thesis [1978] two new conditions with interpretations that are generalizations of Coombs's and Black's conditions: arboricity and quasi-unimodality.

3.3 Romero's Arboricity

A tree is a connected graph without circuit. Imagine then such a tree imbedded in a Euclidean space, as in figure 3.1. Mice, corresponding to the alternatives, and cats, corresponding to criteria, are scattered along the edges of the

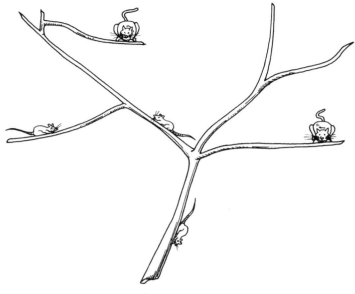

Figure 3.1

imbedded tree. The criteria will rank the alternatives in the same way that the corresponding cats would rank the corresponding mice: from the nearest to the farthest away, crawling along the edges of the tree.

More formally, a tree T imbedded in a Euclidean space (as there is only one path between two points on T), induces a distance function d on the points in T.

Let p_c denote a one-to-one correspondence between the criteria and a first set of points of T called points-criteria, and let p_a denote a one-to-one correspondence between the alternatives and a second set of points of T, called points-alternatives.

If the profile E follows *the arboricity condition,* then for criterion i, the alternative x will be ranked before the alternative y if the distance $d(p_c(i), p_a(x))$ is smaller than $d(p_c(i), p_a(y))$.

Lemma 3.2
If a profile follows the arboricity condition, then, from any triple of alternatives, one is never ranked third of the triple by any criterion.

Proof If the three corresponding mice are on the same path, the result is trivial.

If the shortest paths between the three mice are Y shaped, it is easy to see that the alternative whose corresponding mouse is the nearest to the Y intersection will never be ranked third of the triple in any individual vote.

There is no general test known for this condition. Its applicability seems to be limited to a very special field: determining the location of some public utility in a treelike network from a set of possible locations.

The value of the $F(n)$ corresponding to the arboricity condition is bounded by the value of $F(n)$ corresponding to the single condition: one alternative out of each triple is never ranked last. This upper bound will be computed later.

Arboricity suggests another condition, which we shall call (in order to be coherent with what follows) arboricity-in-the-mirror. Suppose that the mice rank the cats. The best cat would be, of course, the one that is the furthest away! This condition, which looks like a joke, makes sense, however in searching for a less competitive environment. In the model, then, the mice are possible competitors and the cats are possible locations. Each criterion would rank the locations from the best to the worst with regard to the corresponding competitor.

3.4   Romero's Quasi-Unimodality

This is a generalization of Black's condition with two reference orders. It has a loose connection with the conditions introduced by Black and Newing [1951].

Its definition will be first suggested through an example: consider a set of current research projects in a university. The president has the opportunity to grant extra funding to those projects that are confronted with unforeseen difficulties.

Two vice-presidents with different special interests are asked to establish a ranking of the projects, ranking first (i.e., best) the project that is most feasible under the present state of affairs (therefore the most likely to be completed without any additional allocation).

Suppose that the members of the board consider the two vice-presidents as equally competent in their specialties, and yet the two rankings given by them are very different. The board will need to rank the projects according to their expected monetary requirements; hence the members will rank on their ballots as least needy (i.e., last) one of those ranked first by the vice-presidents; they will indicate as second neediest one of the remaining "best" ones, and so forth.

The profile consisting of the ballots of the members of the board will be said to follow the quasi-unimodality condition.

More formally, let R_1 and R_2 be two reference orders on X.

Definition 3.2 (Quasi-unimodality)
Consider a criterion K in a profile E. Let Y be the set of the p last objects according to this criterion, and $X - Y$ the set of the remaining objects. Then, if the $(p + 1)$th alternative in K from the bottom is either the last alternative in $R_1(X - Y)$

or the last alternative in $R_2(X - Y)$, and if this is true for any K in E and any p, then E follows the quasi-unimodality condition.

Clearly, if R_1 and R_2 are opposite, the condition is identical to Black's condition. But it is easy to check in the following example that this is not true in general. Consider the profile $\{(dcba),(acbd)\}$. It is trivially quasi-unimodal for the reference orders $dcba$ and $acbd$ but is not unimodal. If it were unimodal, its reference order would begin and end with a and d, which leaves four possibilities: $dbca$, $acbd$, $dcba$, $abcd$. But the first criterion, $dcba$, cannot accept any of the two first ones for reference order in a Blackian profile. And the same is true for the second criterion and the two last potential reference orders.

Lemma 3.3
Given a profile E following the quasi-unimodality condition, for each triple of alternatives, one will not be ranked last of the three by any criterion.

The proof of this proposition, which implies the transitivity of the majority method, is straightforward.

Let us suppose that the best ranked object of the triple is x in the first reference order, and y in the second. Then z will never be ranked last of the triple because x or y has been ranked previously as the last one.

Now, if both reference orders rank the same alternative first, then the other two alternatives will never be the last in any ballot.

Of course, no algorithm to test this condition has been derived. Its application—a priori—is exceptional because it implies choosing at each step "the best" among the two "best" in R_1 or in R_2 without taking as "best" the object that would have, for instance, the lowest average rank.

It is clear, from the algorithm that defined this condition, that the maximum number of different individual rankings in a profile following the condition is bounded by 2^{n-1}.

Romero, in his dissertation, presented another interpretation, which does not seem realistic, but which perhaps can provide a cue for some better ones. Consider a set of patients in an intensive care unit. Two major disorders have been killing the patients in this unit: heart and kidney failures. A cardiologist "objectively" ranks the patients according to the state of their hearts; a urologist does the same according to the state of their kidneys. This information is then given to the staff, which is then asked to rank the patients from the most to the least fragile.

Given the fact that complete failure of *either* the heart *or* the kidneys can be fatal, Romero supposes that each member of the staff will rank as most vulnerable one of the two worst ranked patients: the worst on the cardiologist's ranking and the worst on the urologist's ranking. Then, in order to rank the second worst one, the members of the staff would delete the first already ranked and proceed in the same way with the remaining patients, etc.

This model is probably inexact, because of synergy effects: having a rank on one of the two scales is probably weighted by the rank on the other scale. Let us check that this condition can clearly give way to variations, the different rankings being made from the worst to the best or from the best to the worst arbitrarily. For some cases, one alternative of each triple will never be the last; for the others, one alternative of each triple will never be the first. We shall see that these are both cases which imply the transitivity of the majority method.

3.5 Arrow's and Black's Single-Peakedness

These first four conditions all have one common point; they are all particular cases of the Arrow-Black condition (Arrow [1963]) called single-peakedness.

Definition 3.3 (Single-peakedness)
For any triple of alternatives $\{x,y,z\}$ one alternative at least will never be ranked as third of the set by any criterion.

This purely algebraic condition seems to lack any psychological interpretation pertinent for our final purpose. However, it looks, of course, as if it should be much more generous in terms of diversity allowed to the criteria than those described above. The following result by Köhler [1978] shows that, paradoxically, no more diversity is granted by single-peakedness than by its three last particular cases that we have just described.

D. Romero was among the first ones who mentioned clearly ([1978]) that single-peakedness was not unimodality: our last example, trivially single peaked (as for any triple of alternatives, one at least cannot be the last in any of the *two* criteria), does not follow Black's condition.

A slightly redundant remark has to be made here. In all the previous conditions, a reference structure was common to all the criteria: a numerical axis in Coombs's condition, a tree imbedded in a Euclidean space in arboricity, one or two linear orders for the others. In our expression of Arrow-Black's condition, the common "agreement" is not global, but given on the triples only. One can even say that the prohibited ordered triples are not given, but that, a profile E being given, the exhibition of any set of prohibitions such that for any triple of alternatives T, one is never third in $E(T)$, will ensure the respect of the condition.

For this reason, our diversity index should be considered as a measure of freedom only with precautions. Imagine that the criteria are voters. Imagine that they vote in sequence, and that the president, who does not vote, gives to each of them just before they cast their ballot the effective list of the ballots they can cast without breaking the condition. Then, the first voter would have an unrestricted list, and the list of the restrictions on individual freedom would only increase simultaneously with the number of different votes already expressed.

This is one of the reasons why we tried to avoid the use of the word freedom, which conveys indeed too many ideological connotations, and preferred the term degree of diversity to denote the ratio $F(n)/n!$.

Theorem 3.3
For the Arrow-Black condition $F(n) = 2^{n-1}$.

Proof (1) Consider a profile E for which, for any $Y \subset X$, $|Y| \geqslant 3$, the number of the objects ranked last in the $\theta_i(Y)$ is at most two. Then, if Y is any triple, this implies that one of its three elements will never be ranked last: which is the Arrow-Black condition. (2) Suppose now that there exists in some profile E', a set of $Y \subset X$ with $|Y| \geqslant 3$ such that the set of objects ranked last in the θ_i contain at least three objects, x,y,z among them. Then, for the triple $\{x,y,z\}$ Arrow-Black's condition would not be satisfied. Hence, if Arrow-Black's condition is satisfied, for all $Y \subset X$, $|Y| \geqslant 3$ the set of the objects ranked last in the θ_i contains two objects at most. (3) Construct now the ranking given by any particular criterion. If its last object is chosen first, it will have the choice, not over all the elements in X, but, as we have just seen, in fact only over two. Let z be the chosen object. The object with the second worst rank, among the remaining set $X - z$, can, in fact, be only one from a set of two, and so on. Hence $F(n) = 2^{n-1}$.

Another result should now be made equally explicit.

Theorem 3.4
Arrow-Black's condition ensures the transitivity of majority voting.

Proof   Consider a triple $\{x,y,z\}$ and suppose that majority rule ("with an odd number of criteria") does not give a transitive result but that for strictly more than 50% of the criteria x is better than y, y better than z, and z better than x. That would mean, in the necessarily nonempty pairwise intersections of these strict majorities, that one ballot has x before y before z, one ballot has y before z before x, and one ballot has z before x before y. Thus, E would not follow the Arrow-Black condition.

Then, for the triple $\{x,y,z\}$ the Arrow-Black condition would not be satisfied. Hence, if the Arrow-Black condition is satisfied, for all $Y \subset X$, $|Y| \geq 3$ the set of objects ranked last in the θ_i contains two objects at most.

We can conclude from this that some conditions with meaningful interpretations are particular cases of the Arrow-Black condition of single-peakedness. But the restrictions imposed on the profiles by single-peakedness are such that these conditions will not allow us to believe that the majority method will be able to solve the ordering problem on which we focused this book. This was already suggested by the papers due to Kramer [1973, 1976].

We shall however, select some of the purely algebraic conditions, generalizing the conditions with interpretation. Mathematical considerations will then lead us to abandon our last unrealistic illusions about the majority method.

Over the next three chapters, the extremely limited domain of efficacy of the majority method will be outlined with some precision. This will give a legitimate tool to the operations researcher. He will be able to diagnose the rare cases in which the majority method will be a successful model for his multicriterion ranking problems.

4 More Conditions with Interpretation

Desiring to expand as much as possible the set of conditions of transitivity for the majority method with interpretation, Köhler [1978], Romero [1978], and Raynaud [1981a,b] investigated a little further, mathematically speaking, the current purely algebraic conditions: this and the next chapter thereby have a more technical emphasis.

The motivation for going further was merely that the Black-Arrow condition was so precipitously restrictive that it could not be considered as a way truly to restore the efficacy of the majority method for real multicriterion decision-making. As described in chapters 1 and 2, the method for a large number of criteria and alternatives must give a total ordering for a large set of projects. The "efficacy" of the method is not that expected from a method to be used by a committee: in order to be efficacious, our method *needs* transitivity *and* robustness.

4.1 The C_{ij} Conditions

We can further explore the set of conditions of transitivity for majority rule that offer algorithmic interpretations by using particular cases of the condition $Ref(i,j,v)$ in Köhler [1978]; from them, one can derive nine conditions for transitivity of the method of majority decision that all possess a generating algorithm with a sociological or economic interpretation. Those previously described appear in this structure. Some others, new at least in their algorithmic form, suggest explanations for some efficacious multi-criterion decisions.

In this chapter,

• X denotes a finite set of objects called alternatives.

• E (or $E(X)$) denotes a profile on X, i.e., a sequence $\theta_1, \ldots, \theta_N$ of total orders on X called criteria.

• $\forall Y \subseteq X$, $\theta_m(Y)$ is the restriction of θ_m to only the alternatives in Y and $E(Y)$ is the restriction of the profile E to the alternatives of Y, i.e., the sequence of the $\theta_m(Y)$.

• A CTMM is a Condition for Transitivity of the Method of Majority decision.

• Every CTMM in the chapter will consist of the prohibition of certain profiles and $F^C(n) = n!f(n)$ will be equal to the maximum number of different rankings in a profile satisfying condition C.

If R is a given reference order, and i, j, ν are three integers such that $0 < i \le \nu + 1$, $0 < j \le \nu + 1$, then Köhler's [1978] condition Ref(i,j,ν) says, "$\forall Y \subseteq X$, $|Y| = \nu + 1$, the ith alternative in $R(Y)$ is never in the jth rank in any $\theta_m(Y)$."

We shall specify here the value of $\nu = 2$. Nine conditions Ref can then be written, i and j being able to take the values 1, 2, 3. These conditions will be denoted C_{ij} and, R being fixed, will depend only on i and j.

The reader familiar with voting theory will not be surprised to know that the C_{ij} are particular cases of the celebrated Ward's CTMM, which is purely algebraic.

Ward's condition [1965]
A profile is said to follow Ward's condition if and only if one cannot find three alternatives a, b, c, in X and three

criteria $\theta_1, \theta_2, \theta_3$ such that

$\theta_1(a,b,c) = a, b, c,$

$\theta_2(a,b,c) = b, c, a,$

$\theta_3(a,b,c) = c, a, b.$

This condition is often described by saying that "there is no Condorcet triple in E."

Theorem 4.1
Ward's condition ensures the transitivity of the majority rule for any odd number of criteria.

Proof Let E be a profile following Ward's condition. If strictly more than 50% of the criteria rank a before b, and strictly more than 50% b before c, it is not possible that strictly more than 50% of the criteria rank c before a.

If it were so, on the contrary, one would have at least one criterion ranking a before b before c, another one ranking b before c before a and a third one ranking c before a before b, and E would not follow Ward's condition.

Lemma 4.1
C_{ij} is a particular case of Ward's condition.

Proof For every triple $T(a,b,c)$ two different permutant Latin squares can be found in $E(T)$:

$a\ b\ c$ $b\ a\ c$
$b\ c\ a$ *and* $a\ c\ b$
$c\ a\ b$ $c\ b\ a$

Any of the C_{ij} forbids at least one line in each of the two possible Latin squares (trivially checked by mere enumeration).

4.2   Operations on the CTMMs

Certain relations between the C_{ij} can enhance the correspondences between the interpretations they suggest. In
order to describe the correspondences between the properties of the C_{ij}, we need to recall some tools.

Definition 4.1 (Romero [1978])
Let C be a CTMM. We say that E follows $\bar{C}$ or C-in-the-
mirror if the mirror images of the rankings of E follow C.
(This is identical to what P. C. Fishburn [1973] calls dual or
converse orders and profiles.)

It is trivial to remark that $\bar{C}$ is a CTMM. If $\bar{\theta}_n$ denotes the
mirror image of θ_m, $\bar{E}$ denotes the profile $(\bar{\theta}_1, \bar{\theta}_2, \ldots, \bar{\theta}_N)$. In
addition, $F^C(n)$, the maximum number of different values
for the criteria in a profile following condition C, is equal to
$F^{\bar{C}}(n)$.

Definition 4.2
Let R be a reference order on X and θ a total order on X.
With any pair (θ, R) one can associate a matrix $M_R(\theta)$ with
n^2 elements denoted P_{ij}, $P_{ij} = 1 \leftrightarrow$ the ith alternative in R is
the jth alternative in θ. $P_{ij} = 0$ in all other cases.

If $M_R^t(\theta)$ denotes the transpose of $M_R(\theta)$, $M_R^t(\theta)$ is equally
a permutation matrix and can be written $M_R(\theta^t)$ in a unique
way. θ^t is the transposed order of θ; $E^t = (\theta_1^t, \ldots, \theta_N^t)$ is the
transposed profile of $E = (\theta_1, \ldots, \theta_N)$.

The transposition operation has been employed by various authors under different names: inversion, duality, etc.
For more details on definitions 4.1 and 4.3 and lemma 4.3,
the reading of Köhler [1978] will be enlightening.

Definition 4.3
E follows the CTMM C^t if and only if E^t follows C.

Lemma 4.2
$F^{C^t}(n) = F^C(n)$.

Proof Trivial, from the fact that transposition is a bijection of the set of total orders into itself.

Lemma 4.3
$C_{ij} = C_{ji}^t \; (= (C_{ij}^t)^t) = C_{i,4-j}$.

Proof (1) Consider θ in a profile E following C_{ij}. Consider the 3×3 submatrix of $M_R(\theta)$ corresponding to the alternatives (x,y,z) of a triple T. If, for T, the jth alternative in $R(T)$ is not the ith in θ, then the corresponding (j,i)th element in the submatrix is zero. If one transposes $M_R(\theta)$, the considered submatrix still corresponds to the alternatives in T, but the submatrix has itself been transposed, and it is its (i,j)th element, which is a zero. As R has stayed the same, in θ^t one can say that the ith alternative is never in the jth rank. (2) Consider E following C_{ij}. Let T be a triple of X, and x be its ith alternative in $R(T)$. Let $\theta \in E$. It is clear in $\bar{\theta}(T)$, x

- will never be in position 1, if it was never in position 3 in θ,

- will never be in position 2, if it was never in position 2 in θ,

- will never be in position 3, if it was never in position 1 in θ.

The result follows.

Lemma 4.4
$C_{4-i,j}$ (where $i, j \leq 3$), with reference order R, is the same CTMM as C_{ij}, but with $\bar{R}$ as its reference order.

The proof is left to the reader.

In what follows, operation r will denote the operation obtained on a profile by reversal of its reference order.

4.3 The Three Components of the Graph of the C_{ij} (Raynaud [1981a])

Let us now consider the nine C_{ij} as the vertices of a graph G. An arc of this graph will go from C_{ij} to C_{lk} if and only if C_{lk} can be obtained from C_{ij}

- either by the mirror operation: $C_{lk} = C_{ij} = C_{i(4-j)}$,
- or by the transpose operation: $C_{lk} = C_{ij}^{t} = C_{ji}$,
- or by operation r: $C_{kl} = C_{(4-i)j}$.

Because of the idempotence of these three operators, G is symmetric. It hence has three types of edges, respectively, denoted m, t, r, and exhibits, as shown in figure 4.1, three connected components.

1. *The first connected component* deals with already known conditions. C_{23} is Black's condition as described previously. Hence $\bar{C}_{23} = C_{21}$. For each profile following C_{21} there exists a unique corresponding profile E following C_{23}, obtained by reversing the rankings.

Consider now C_{12} and the reference order R. The first alternative in R, which is the first alternative in all of the triples to which it belongs, cannot be in the middle of any triple. It must then be ranked by the criteria as the best or worst alternative. When this is done, the criteria will rank the second object in the best or worst remaining rank, etc. This algorithm can, of course, describe the arrival of messages that are going to be classified for treatment in two different piles in each of which the priority is "first-come, first served"; the reference order R is simply the order in which the alternatives reach the judge. In other words, each judge only indicates a partition of the set of alterna-

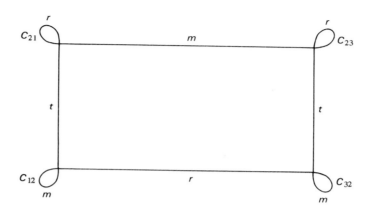

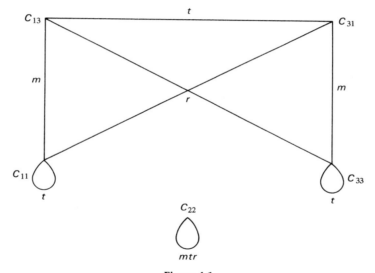

Figure 4.1

tives, and the reference order then plays a role in priorities that the judge does not master.

Imagine, for instance, that the reference order means a ranking according to the share of the budget spent by each of the alternatives; the judges could then be asked to rank the projects in two classes: the probably feasible and the probably unfeasible. Majority rule will make very coherent judgments on the projects in accordance with the strategy of the firm: if feasible, the most expensive is the best; if likely to be unfeasible, the most expensive is the worst!

This condition could be called, clearly, "bipartition with a reference ordering."

An algorithm to obtain the unknown reference order(s) for which a given profile might satisfy the condition is easily derived from the fact that, $\forall Y \subset X$, the first alternative in $R(Y)$ will be ranked exclusively first or last in $E(Y)$.

Hence, the algorithm can proceed as follows:

(1) Let X be the set of remaining alternatives at the starting step.

(2) At any step, let Y be the set of remaining alternatives. Consider $E(Y)$; if no alternative appears only at the last and first ranks, the problem has no solution. If one does, say, x, delete it from Y, and rank it as the next alternative in R.

(3) $Y - x$ becomes henceforth the set of remaining alternatives. If it is nonvoid, return to (2). If it is void, the algorithm is finished, and all the solutions obtained for R will be satisfying ones.

C_{32} would of course be the same as C_{12} after reversing the reference order, which represents a mere convention.

2. *The second component* covers conditions with very similar interpretations, obtained from one another merely by the use of operations m and r, which are trivial.

No algorithm describing the ranking along one criterion

has yet been derived from these conditions. Let us consider, for instance, C_{13}. The first alternative in the reference order is the first for all the triples to which it belongs. This implies that its rank, in any criterion, is necessarily 1 or 2. Then, in order to build the ranking of one criterion, one can

(1) Consider the restriction of the reference order to the not yet ranked alternatives. Take the first one. Rank it in one of the two remaining best ranks.

(2) If there is more than one alternative left, repeat step (1).

A corresponding algorithm for C_{11} would be obtained by changing "best" to "worst" (for C_{31} change in addition "first" to "last").

If you suspect a profile E to follow C_{13}, it will not be difficult to find if there exists any corresponding reference order.

(i) Write out all your rankings one under the other. Read the two first columns in order to see whether one alternative is always ranked in the first or second rank. If none, the problem has no solution.

(ii) If any, it is a feasible candidate for the first rank of the reference order. Store it as your first ranked alternative, delete it from your data and proceed with what remains.

Clearly here again $F^{C_{31}}(n) = F^{C_{13}}(n) = F^{C_{11}}(n) = F^{C_{33}}(n) = 2^{n-1}$.

Conditions C_{31}, C_{13}, C_{11}, or C_{33} can be interpreted as a chronological process in which each alternative introduced will in turn be classified as first or second class. If it is first class, it will take the first remaining free rank; if it is second class, it will leave the first rank free and go to the next free one.

3. *Then remains the original C_{22}* (Raynaud [1981]). Why is it so original? You would think that, given a reference order

R, a maximum of 2^{n-1} different rankings can be numbered in the profiles following C_{22}. It is at least true for $X = \{a,b,c\}$: if (a,b,c) is the reference order, $\{bac, bca, cab, acb\} = E_{max}^3$.

If you now try to obtain by enumeration $F(4)$ for a profile satisfying C_{22}, you can do it by introducing in the previous orders of E_{max}^3 a fourth alternative, say, d, then deleting those orders containing unallowed triples. This gives

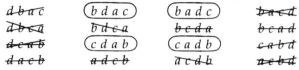
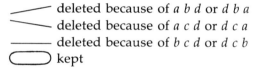

Legend:

⎯⎯ deleted because of $a\ b\ d$ or $d\ b\ a$
⎯⎯ deleted because of $a\ c\ d$ or $d\ c\ a$
⎯⎯ deleted because of $b\ c\ d$ or $d\ c\ b$
⊂⊃ kept

And now, if you try to introduce a fifth alternative e, you obtain

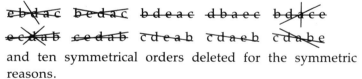

and ten symmetrical orders deleted for the symmetric reasons.

Legend:

⎯⎯ deleted because of $e\ d\ a$ or $a\ d\ e$
⎯⎯ deleted because of $b\ d\ e$ or $e\ d\ b$
⎯⎯ deleted because of $c\ d\ e$ or $e\ d\ c$

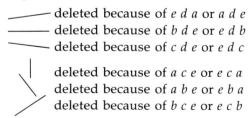

deleted because of $a\ c\ e$ or $e\ c\ a$
deleted because of $a\ b\ e$ or $e\ b\ a$
deleted because of $b\ c\ e$ or $e\ c\ b$

In other words, there is *no* profile on X, with $|X| > 4$, that satisfies C_{22}. The conjecture now is, This has a nice economic interpretation!

The study of these conditions with reference orders and some kind of interpretation drove us toward another more algebraic class of generalizations of Black's condition and led us to a classical error, which the next chapter will repair.

5 Paradoxical Results from Inada's Conditions for Majority Rule

In a well known paper, K.-I. Inada [1964] generalized Arrow-Black's single-peakedness. He defined two new conditions (often quoted as Inada's conditions) plus a third one, the bipartition condition, which he thought to be equivalent to one of the first two, the not-in-the-middle (NITM) condition. Morton [1966] was the first to doubt this property. We show in this chapter that the bipartition condition is strictly contained in the not-in-the-middle condition. This investigation will then allow us to show that these conditions do not allow more diversity than does single-peakedness.

5.1 Inada's Conditions

Definition 5.1
E follows *single-cavedness* if for all triples $\{x,y,z\}$, one of the three alternatives is never ranked first in any $\theta_i(\{xyz\})$. Single-cavedness, of course, generalizes C_{11}, C_{21}, and C_{31}. It is, of course, nothing other than single-peakedness in-the-mirror.

Definition 5.2
E follows the *not-in-the-middle* condition (in short NITM condition) if for all triples $\{x,y,z\}$, one of the three alternatives is never ranked second in any $\theta_i(\{xyz\})$.

The NITM condition, of course, generalizes C_{12}, C_{32}, and C_{22}. This probably explains why the calculation of $F(n)$ for the NITM condition was not easy: we pointed out the irregularity of C_{22} in the previous chapter.

In order to define the bipartition condition in a clear and simple way, we need some additional notation:

• Let Y and Z denote two nonintersecting subsets of X.

• Let θ be any ranking of X and $\theta(Y)$ (respectively, $\theta(Z)$) be the restriction of θ to the alternatives in Y (respectively, Z).

• Then $\theta(Y)\theta(Z)$ (respectively, $\theta(Z)\theta(Y)$) will denote the ranking of $Y \cup Z$ in which all the alternatives in Y(respectively, Z) outrank all the alternatives in Z (respectively, Y) and such that its restriction to only the alternatives in Y (respectively, Z) be precisely $\theta(Y)$ (respectively, $\theta(Z)$).

Definition 5.3
E follows the *bipartition condition* if, for any $Y \subset X$, there exists a partition of Y into two nonempty subsets Y_1, Y_2 such that for any criterion θ, either $\theta(Y) = \theta(Y_1)\theta(Y_2)$ or $\theta(Y) = \theta(Y_2)\theta(Y_1)$.

As an intuitive formulation, one can say that for any subset Y and X, there exists a bipartition of Y into Y_1, Y_2 such that, for any criterion, either all the alternatives in Y_1 outrank all the alternatives in Y_2 or all the alternatives in Y_2 outrank all the alternatives in Y_1.

The reader could wonder if the bipartition is clearly different from single-peakedness. The following example will show it explicitly. Consider the profile on $X = \{a,b,c,d\}$ given by the three orders *abcd*, *adbc*, *dbca*, denoted 1, 2, 3, respectively.

The profile follows the bipartition condition: a first bipartition can be made into $\{a\}$, $\{b,c,d\}$, then $\{b,c,d\}$ can be cut into $\{d\}$, $\{b,c\}$. Consequently, for any Y included in X, there exists a bipartition of Y satisfying the condition.

Now consider the triples

- for $\{a,b,c\}$, a is last in 3, b is last in 2, and c is last in 1;
- for $\{a,b,d\}$, a is last in 3, b is last in 2, and d is last in 1;
- for $\{a,c,d\}$, a is last in 3, c is last in 2, and d is last in 1;
- for $\{b,c,d\}$, b is last in 2, c is last in 3, and d is last in 1.

Hence E does not satisfy the single-peakedness condition.

5.2 Relationship between the Bipartition Condition and the NITM Condition

Theorem 5.1
If a profile E follows the bipartition condition, then it follows the NITM condition.

Proof Consider any triple $\{x,y,z\}$ of alternatives. As E follows the bipartition condition, there exists a bipartition denotable without loss of generality $Y_1 = \{x\}$, $Y_2 = \{y,z\}$ such that all the possible rankings for the criteria are

$$xyz \quad \text{or} \quad xzy \quad \text{or} \quad zyx \quad \text{or} \quad yzx.$$

In these rankings, x is never ranked second: one alternative is never in the middle.

Lemma 5.1
Any profile containing only two criteria follows the NITM condition.

Proof Trivial.

Lemma 5.2 (Raynaud [1979])
$K = \{abcd, bdac\}$ is a profile that follows the NITM condition but not the bipartition condition.

Proof   One can list three possible bipartitions that would allow the ranking *abcd*:

- $\{\{a\}\{bcd\}\}$,
- $\{\{ab\}\{cd\}\}$,
- $\{\{abc\}\{d\}\}$.

However, none of them allows the second ranking. The result follows then straightforwardly from definition 5.3.

Definition 5.4
We shall say that E' is a *subprofile* of E if it is a profile obtained by restricting a subset of the criteria to a subset of the alternatives in E.

Clearly, by lemma 5.2, if K is a subprofile of E, E cannot follow the bipartition condition. Hence, among the profiles satisfying the NITM condition one can point out two subsets:

1. the subset of the profiles satisfying the bipartition condition (and thus not having K as a subprofile),

2. the subset of the profiles containing K as a subprofile.

With a little combinatorial effort, one can derive the fact that these are the only two possibilities.

Theorem 5.2 (Raynaud [1981a])
Any profile satisfying the NITM condition must either contain K as a subprofile or follow the bipartition condition.

Proof   The theorem is trivially true for a profile on three alternatives.

Suppose that it is true for $|X| = 3, 4, \ldots, n-1$ and becomes untrue for $|X| = n$. This implies the existence of a profile E on a set X of n alternatives that satisfies the NITM condition, does not contain K, and does not satisfy the bipartition condition, but such that all its subprofiles on

$(n - 1)$ alternatives satisfy the bipartition condition. Let $\lambda \in X$ and let E' be the restriction of E to $X - \lambda$. There exist Z and Y such that any criterion θ_m in E' ranks all the alternatives in Z before all the alternatives in Y or all the alternatives in Y before all the alternatives in Z. Throughout this proof, we shall write, without ambiguity, that $\theta_m(X - \lambda) = ZY$ or YZ, where Z (respectively, Y) will denote by extension a ranking of the alternatives in Z (respectively, Y).

If Y^λ (respectively, Z^λ) denotes a ranking including all the alternatives in Y (respectively, Z) plus λ, λ being *not* an extreme in the rankings, E will a priori possibly contain five types of rankings, namely:

1. λZY or $YZ\lambda$,

2. $Z^\lambda Y$ or YZ^λ,

3. $Z\lambda Y$ or $Y\lambda Z$,

4. ZY^λ or $Y^\lambda Z$,

5. $ZY\lambda$ *or* λYZ.

A. Clearly, a criterion cannot yield rankings of one type only, because in that case, E would follow the bipartition condition.

B. If a profile contains rankings of the types 1, 2, 4, or 1, 3, 4, there exists for this profile y, an element of Y, and z, an element of Z, such that $\{\lambda, y, z\}$ does not respect the NITM condition.

For symmetry reasons, it is equally true of the types 4, 5, 2, and 5, 3, 2. Then any profile with at least four types of rankings will contain at least three criteria belonging to a noncompatible set; for instance, a profile containing rankings of types 1, 2, 3, 4, will contain a criterion of type 1, another of type 2, and another of type 4—and these three types together are not compatible with the NITM condition.

Consider now a profile containing the combination 2, 3,

4, or any from among 1, 2, 5; 1, 3, 5; 1, 4, 5. There would clearly exist another triple $\{z,y,\lambda\}$ for which the NITM condition would not be respected. Hence E cannot contain criteria giving 5 or even 4 different types of ranking, since $\{\lambda yz\}$ would not then follow the NITM condition.

Among the profiles with three different types of ranking only $\{1,2,3\}$ and $\{3,4,5\}$ would be, for the same reason, feasible combinations. But $\{Y,Z + \lambda\}$, in the first case, and $\{Z,Y + \lambda\}$, in the second, would point out bipartitions for E.

C. From all this, E may contain rankings of only two types. Combinations $(1,2)$, $(1,3)$, $(1,5)$, $(2,3)$, $(3,4)$, $(3,5)$, $(4,5)$ are all combinations exhibiting a trivial bipartition. Three only remain a priori feasible: $(1,4)$, $(2,4)$ and $(2,5)$. Note that $(1,4)$ and $(2,5)$ are symmetrical, so only $(1,4)$ and $(2,4)$ need be studied.

D. Case of $(1,4)$. If $\{Y_1 \cup \lambda, Y_2\}$ is the bipartition of $Y \cup \lambda$ ensured by the recurrence hypothesis, if $\{Z_1 \cup \lambda, Z_2\}$ is the bipartition of $Z \cup \lambda$ ensured by the recurrence hypothesis, criteria of type 1 will rank λ, then Z_1, then Z_2 then Y_1 then Y_2 or backward, while criteria of type 4 will rank either Z_2 then Z_1 then $Y_1 \cup \lambda$ then Y_2 or Z_2 then Z_1 then Y_2 then $Y_1 \cup \lambda$ or in the reverse orders.

This last fourth pattern necessarily appears. If the rankings of type 4 all had Y_2 at an extremity, this would imply a bipartition between Y_2 and the rest.

Hence, at least one criterion ranked Z_2 then Z_1 then Y_2 then $Y_1 \cup \lambda$ (or the reverse), in which one recalls that λ cannot be the extreme. Let us now consider $z \in Z$, y_1 in Y_1 ranked extreme in one of these last criteria, $y_2 \in Y_2$. We are certain of the presence of one criterion ranking λ then z then y_1 then y_2 (or the reverse) and of another ranking $zy_2\lambda y_1$ (or the reverse). This is nothing else but K.

E. Case of $(2,4)$. With the same notation, the possible

rankings of type 2 can be chosen from among the four subsets

$$Z_2\{Z_1 \cup \lambda\}Y_1Y_2 \qquad Y_2Y_1\{Z_1 \cup \lambda\}Z_2$$

and

$$\{Z_1 \cup \lambda\}Z_2Y_1Y_2 \qquad Y_2Y_1Z_2\{Z_1 \cup \lambda\};$$

and the possible rankings of type 4 can be chosen among the four subsets:

$$Z_2Z_1\{Y_1 \cup \lambda\}Y_2 \qquad Y_2\{Y_1 \cup \lambda\}Z_1Z_2$$

and

$$Z_2Z_1Y_2\{Y_1 \cup \lambda\} \qquad \{Y_1 \cup \lambda\}Y_2Z_1Z_2.$$

In any ranking of type 2, Y_2 is extreme. Therefore among the rankings of type 4, at least one ranking from among either $Z_2Z_1Y_2\{Y_1 \cup \lambda\}$ or its reverse must be chosen in order to avoid a bipartition $\{Y_2, Y_2^c\}$, where the superscript "c" denotes "complement." Conversely, in order to avoid a bipartition $\{Z_2, Z_2^c\}$ ranking from among $\{Z_1 \cup \lambda\}Z_2Y_1Y_2$ or its reverse must be chosen.

Call these two sets of rankings α and β, respectively. Now let y_1 be the extreme of a ranking in α and z_1 an extreme of a ranking in β, $y_2 \in Y_2$, $z_2 \in Z_2$; the profile will then necessarily exhibit one of the four subprofiles:

$$z_2z_1y_2\lambda y_1, \qquad z_1\lambda z_2y_1y_2,$$
$$z_2z_1y_2\lambda y_1, \qquad y_2y_1z_2\lambda z_1,$$
$$y_1\lambda y_2z_1z_2, \qquad z_1\lambda z_2y_1y_2,$$
$$y_1\lambda y_2z_1z_2, \qquad y_2y_1z_2\lambda z_1.$$

In the first case $\quad z_2z_1y_2\lambda, \qquad z_1\lambda z_2y_2 \qquad$ is K,

in the second case $\quad y_2z_2\lambda z_1, \qquad z_2z_1y_2\lambda \qquad$ is K,

in the third case $\quad z_1\lambda z_2y_2, \qquad \lambda y_2z_1z_2 \qquad$ is K,

in the fourth case $\quad y_2y_1z_2\lambda, \qquad y_1\lambda y_2z_2 \qquad$ is K.

The "objective" bipartition of any set with cardinality larger than 2 seems, in fact, to occur very rarely in nature—as probably do any of Inada's conditions. Their real merit may lie, rather, in the fact that they drive toward some synthetic conditions (very simple) of purely algebraic nature, but which allow synthetic proofs and which will be presented in the next chapter.

5.3 The Degree of Diversity Allowed by Inada's Conditions

Some final remarks still remain to be made; we have to determine whether or not the NITM condition is more generous than single-peakedness and single-cavedness in terms of degrees of diversity.

Theorem 5.3
The maximum number of different rankings in a profile following bipartition condition is $2^{|X|-1}$.

Proof (By induction on $|X|$) The result is trivial for $|X| = 2$. Let us suppose it's true until $|X| = n - 1$. If, now, $|X| = n$, we know that there exists a bipartition of X in $\{X_1, X_2\}$ such that, in any ranking by a criterion, either all the alternatives in X_1 outrank all the alternatives in X_2 or all the alternatives in X_2 outrank all the alternatives in X_1. If $|X_1| = m$ and $|X| = p$, then $F(n) = 2^{m-1} \times 2^{p-1} \times 2 = 2^{n-1}$.

Theorem 5.4
For any profile (with $|X| = n$), 2^{n-1} different rankings at most are permitted to the criteria. But if such a profile contains K, 2^{n-2} different rankings only are permitted.

Proof Let us first remark that, in the progressive process of building a profile on n objects following the NITM condition, a new alternative added to those in Y can be, in each ranking of $E(Y)$, introduced at two different ranks at most. In order to verify that this is true, suppose that, on the contrary, there would exist one ranking, θ in $E(Y)$ where a new alternative x could possibly be introduced at three different ranks $i < j < k$. Let y be the ith in $\theta(Y)$ and z the jth. $E(Y + x)$ would then include

θ_1, ranking x before y before z,

θ_2, ranking y before x before z,

θ_3, ranking y before z before x.

This is impossible, because the triple $\{x,y,z\}$ would then not follow the NITM condition.

Now suppose that E contains K, or, more precisely, that it contains the four alternatives $\{a,b,c,d\}$, and the rankings *abcd* and *bdac*. Can any other ranking be added to these without breaking the NITM conditions? These additional rankings will have to respect the four following restrictions:

out of $\{a,b,c\}$, c will never be in the middle,

out of $\{a,b,d\}$, a will never be in the middle,

out of $\{a,c,d\}$, d will never be in the middle,

out of $\{b,c,d\}$, b will never be in the middle.

A mere enumeration of the possibilities will directly lead the reader to *dcba* and *cadb*. These four rankings (which can be written as a symmetric matrix) constitute the largest profile on four objects satisfying the NITM condition and containing K:

abcd,

bdac,

cadb,

dcba.

Clearly $F(4) = 2^2$ for this double condition. Let us then add a new alternative to the first ones—for instance, at the extremities of each of the rankings. It is easy to see that this technique will yield a profile on five objects satisfying the NITM condition and containing K with a maximal number of different rankings. By iteration, this will, of course, allow the statement $F(n) = 2^{n-2}$. When a profile follows the bipartition condition we know that $F(n) = 2^{n-1}$. As the NITM condition implies one of these two exclusive possibilities, the proof of the theorem is completed.

The conclusion of this chapter is that Arrow-Black's and Inada's conditions on triples do not allow more diversity in the rankings belonging to one single profile than the more restrictive looking C_{ij}. As an example, consider a majority voting procedure for a committee where all the individuals are restricted to respect some particular condition of transitivity for the majority method. Suppose, in addition, that each individual ballot is a linear ranking on a finite set of alternatives. Then, the ratio between the maximum number of different ballots an individual is allowed to cast and what would be its value in the total absence of restriction can be considered as a measure of the effective individual freedom granted by this condition. Our last result thus implies that the conditions of transitivity expressed on triples only (Arrow-Black's and Inada's) do not generate any more individual freedom than the C_{ij}.

6

How Restrictive Actually Are the Value Restriction Conditions?

We have advanced far enough to figure out how strong the restrictions have to be on a profile in order to ensure the transitivity of the majority method—essential to its success from the point of view of the decision maker. In order to make these restrictions precise we shall proceed by means of the axiomatic method; the decision scientist would probably think that more axioms should be added to our three—two out of them, alas, are already sufficient to prove the failure of the majority method for our decision purpose. The very loose claim made by these axioms will impose surprisingly drastic limitations on the permitted profiles.

This chapter will begin with the discussion of our three very "generous" axioms, and it will be shown that all of the conditions following these axioms are necessarily special cases of Sen's value restriction condition (Sen [1966]). In the second part, an upper bound for $F(n)$ for the value restriction condition will be derived and its consequences discussed.

6.1   The Value Restriction Condition

6.1.1   In Search of Reasonable Limitation Axioms

We can now describe, based on the psychological considerations developed in part I, acceptable mathematical requirements for limiting conditions. We have extensively
insisted on the fuzziness of the real problems: the sets of
alternatives and criteria are never as well defined and limited as they would be in committee decision-making.
Hence, two requirements, mathematically independent,
appear to be unavoidable.

Axiom 6.1 (Alternativewise robustness)
The restrictions on the set of admissible profiles have to be
such that, if $E(X)$ is an admissible profile, then for all Y
included in X, $E(Y)$ is among the admissible subprofiles. In
other words, deleting or adding alternatives should not
alter the transitivity previously obtained. This axiom, of
course, looks strangely like independence of irrelevant alternatives, but here clearly no alternative is irrelevant: if
now $M(E)$ denotes the result of the application of the majority method to a profile E, $M(E(Y))$ could be different
from the restriction of $M(E(X))$ to only the alternatives in
Y. This will not occur in the most important case: *for the
profiles on which it leads to a transitive result*, the independence of irrelevant alternatives will be satisfied.

We can in addition remark that axiom 6.1 discards many
well-known conditions, such as Blin's multidimensional
consistency [1973].

Axiom 6.2 (Criteriawise robustness)
The restrictions on the set of admissible profiles should be
such that, if $E(X)$ is an admissible profile, the subprofile

$E'(X)$ of $E(X)$ obtained by deletion of an arbitrary number of criteria is itself an admissible profile. Of course, the expression "arbitrary number" means that, if necessary, in addition to the arbitrary number of criteria, another one can be added or deleted (in order to eventually reach a total odd number of criteria).

6.1.2   A Fundamental Result

Definition 6.1 (Sen [1966])
A profile follows a value restriction condition if for any unordered triple T of alternatives, there exists one alternative x and one rank $k \in \{1,2,3\}$ such that, in $E(T)$, x will never be in the kth rank.

Definition 6.2 (Ward [1965])
A profile follows Ward's condition if it contains no Condorcet triple, i.e., no triple of alternatives $\{a,b,c\}$ and no triple of criteria $\{\theta_a, \theta_b, \theta_c\}$ such that

$$\theta_a\{a,b,c\} = a,b,c,$$
$$\theta_b\{a,b,c\} = b,c,a,$$
$$\theta_c\{a,b,c\} = c,a,b.$$

Definition 6.3 (Ward [1965])
An equivalent definition of Ward's condition is as follows: E follows the condition if there is no couple (Y, θ), Y included in X, $|Y| \geq 3$, $Y = \{y_1, \ldots, y_r\}$, and θ being a sequence $\theta_{y_1}, \ldots, \theta_{y_r}$ of criteria such that

$$\theta_{y_1}(Y) = y_1 y_2, \ldots, y_{r-1} y_r,$$
$$\theta_{y_2}(Y) = y_2 y_3, \ldots, y_r y_1,$$
$$\vdots$$
$$\theta_{y_r}(Y) = y_r y_1, \ldots, y_{r-2} y_{r-1}.$$

Lemma 6.1
Definitions 6.2 and 6.3 are equivalent.

Proof If E follows definition 6.3, it is clear that E does not contain any Condorcet triple. Conversely, suppose that E contains no Condorcet triple but that there exists a $Y \subset X$, $Y = \{y_1, \ldots, y_r\}$ with $r > 3$, and a sequence $\theta_{y_1}, \ldots, \theta_{y_r}$ of criteria in E such that

$$\theta_{y_1}(Y) = y_1, \ldots, y_{r-1}y_r,$$
$$\theta_{y_2}(Y) = y_2, \ldots, y_r y_1,$$
$$\vdots$$
$$\theta_{y_r}(Y = y_r y_1, \ldots, y_{r-1}.$$

This is impossible because $T = \{y_1, y_2, y_3\}$ would clearly generate a Condorcet triple as

$$\theta_{y_1}(T) = y_1, y_2, y_3,$$
$$\theta_{y2}(T) = y_2, y_3, y_1,$$
$$\theta_{y_3}(T) = y_3, y_1, y_2.$$

Theorem 6.1
A profile follows Ward's condition if and only if it follows some of the value restriction conditions.

Proof Let $T = \{a, b, c\}$ be a triple of alternatives. If it were a Condorcet triple, there would exist three criteria, say $\theta_a, \theta_b, \theta_c$, such that $\theta_a(T) = abc$, $\theta_b(T) = bca$, and $\theta_c(T) = cab$. Any of the three alternatives a, b, c would be found in any of the three ranks and the value restriction condition would not hold. Hence, if E follows a value restriction condition, it follows Ward's condition.

Let us now suppose that E follows Ward's condition and consider any triple $\{abc\}$. Six rankings of these three alternatives are a priori possible: *abc, bca, cab, acb, cba, bac*. As E follows Ward's condition, one ranking at least among the three first, and one among the three last are prohibited.

It is then trivial to check by mere enumeration that each of these nine cases corresponds to one of the nine possible value restriction conditions on T.

Theorem 6.2
All the CTMMs satisfying axioms 6.1 and 6.2 are particular cases of the value restriction condition, and conversely.

Proof Let C be a condition satisfying the two axioms and E any profile satisfying C. Let $\{a,b,c\}$ be any triple of alternatives and $\{\theta_1,\theta_2,\theta_3\}$ be any triple of criteria. This subprofile, since C follows axioms 6.1 and 6.2, satisfies C and, under the majority method, will lead to a transitive result. This consequence is possible only if the considered subprofile is not a Condorcet triple: hence E satisfies Ward's condition.

Conversely, if E follows Ward's condition, it is trivially still true of any of its subprofiles. As respecting Ward's condition means respecting a value restriction condition, the proof is completed.

Remark 1 All the conditions ensuring the transitivity of the majority method described until now have ensured Ward's condition. One can even say that they make more or less precise, for each triple, the object that has a prohibited ranking and/or the rank that is prohibited.

Remark 2 In the business firm, the rankings of the alternatives along the criteria will likely be performed independently by the official experts for these criteria.

Hence, each of them has to be able to know the exact list of the prohibited rankings in order to be able to rank the alternatives without knowing the rankings of the other experts.

In other words, if we want to apply some particular value restriction condition to an industrial problem, the set of corresponding restrictions has to be formulated a priori and not a posteriori.

6.2   The Failure of the Majority Method

The calculation of $F(n)$ in the case of Ward's condition becomes, of course, an interesting challenge. As far as we know, this challenge has stood for twenty years now and does not seem ready to be overcome. In spite of this, what we already know about $F(n)$ yields some decisive conclusions.

$F(3) = 4$: A fifth ranking could always be placed into a Latin square with some two from among the first four. By mere enumeration (Raynaud [1982]), one easily obtains that $F(4) = 9$, which is more than $2^{n-1} = 8$. But the profiles exhibiting nine *different* rankings of four alternatives and *no* Condorcet triple are very rare: about 1 out of 50,000. It is easy to see that, in general, $F(n) > 2^{n-1}$ because, from any profile quoted in Raynaud [1982] for four alternatives, one can derive a satisfactory profile for 5 by merely adding the new alternative successively at the two extremities of each ranking. Then $F(4 + i) \geqslant 9 \times 2i$. If $n = 4 + i$, $F(n) > 2^{i+3} = 2^{n-1}$. Finding out how much larger is the unsolved part of the problem!

James Abello is presently trying to prove that $F(n) < 2^n$ for $n \geqslant 4$. This strong conjecture is supported by his present partial results (Abello [1981, 1985]). Our conclusions can in fact be derived from a much looser, but very easy to obtain, upper bound for $F(n)$. This bound in some ways confirms what could be inferred from the papers by Kramer [1973, 1976].

Theorem 6.3
If E is a profile following Ward's condition, $F(n) \leqslant 2(n - 1)!$.

Proof   The set of the $n!$ different permutations on the n alternatives can be made according to a list of $(n - 1)!$

circulant matrices, each row of one of these being obtained from the previous one by circular permutation. Each first row of the circulant matrices will begin with the same alternative, say, x_1, while the remainder of the first row will be one of the $(n = 1)!$ different permutations of the set of the $(n - 1)$ remaining alternatives.

Now consider one of these circulant matrices; for instance, if $X = \{x_1, x_2, x_3, \ldots, x_n\}$, our first matrix in the list can be

$$
\begin{array}{cccccc}
x_1 & x_2 & \ldots & x_{n-1} & x_n \\
x_2 & x_3 & \ldots & x_n & x_1 \\
\vdots & \vdots & & \vdots & \vdots \\
x_n & x_1 & \ldots & x_{n-2} & x_{n-1}
\end{array}
$$

Because of Ward's condition, E_n does not contain more than two rankings from among this list of n rankings: if it contained three, say, rows p,g,r with $p < g < r$, then x_p, x_g, x_r and rows p,g,r would show a Condorcet triple.

Hence E_n cannot contain more than $2(n - 1)!$ different rankings.

As $f(n)$, the ratio of the number of restricted to the number of unrestricted rankings, remains smaller than $2/n$, one can say that the proportion of permitted rankings, for each criterion, tends toward zero at least as fast as $2/n$ when n grows infinitely.

This clearly implies that, with the exception of *very* restrictive patterns for the criteria, the majority method will require such limitations in terms of permitted rankings for the criteria that it will not be applicable to our industrial problem.

Conclusion of Part II

Exit the majority method and its conditions of transitivity! But not for long. Getting out of the house through the door, it comes back through the window.

One, in effect, would like to say, Whenever the majority method "applies," i.e., gives an operational result, it should be applied, for all the reasons detailed previously. But this, of course, could lead to all the undesirable intransitivities equally described: on every single pair of alternatives the majority method would, literally speaking, apply. Hence, more limited ambitions are compulsory.

The next highest ambition for an aggregation algorithm is to be Condorcet.

Definition 1
Let $x \in Y \subset X$: x is a *Condorcet winner* out of Y if, $\forall y \in Y$, y $\neq x$, x outranks y for a majority of criteria.

Definition 2
An aggregation algorithm, building a multicriterion ranking, is said to be Condorcet if, at each step, it selects as the next alternative, every time that it exists, the Condorcet winner out of the set of the not yet selected alternatives.

Not being Condorcet, for such an algorithm, would clearly allow strong criticism. In addition, it is clear that, if the majority method applied to the entire profile leads to a transitive result, any Condorcet algorithm will build exactly this result. The importance of this property, in terms of frequency, will be, of course, very tightly bound to the probability of occurrence of a Condorcet winner, whenever the probability distribution for the different profiles is uniform. The evaluation of this probability of occurrence, when the number n of alternatives increases, can be performed using the computation presented by Niemi and Weisberg [1968] of its limit value when the number of criteria tends to infinity (by odd values).

Number of alternatives	Frequency of a Condorcet winner
3	.9123
4	.8245
5	.7487
6	.6848
7	.6308
8	.5849
9	.5455
10	.5113

Ten alternatives can be considered as a current value for n in industrial examples: dealing with some Condorcet winners in a row will be very likely in practice, even if the majority method on the whole profile would lead to intransitive results. Applying the majority method locally is in no way theoretical. Conversely, the need for efficient algorithms applicable to more confused profiles is an open field of research. These methods will have to generalize the majority method, and with profiles where it would not be accurate, they will satisfy less demanding axiomatic systems.

The identifications and evaluations of these methods will be the subject of our third part.

Part III

Introduction to Part III

Our purpose, now, is to identify multicriterion ranking methods, defined on purely ordinal data, that would be identical to the majority method if it were applicable. In addition, these methods should not be "too far from it" in precisely those large scale problems where the majority method leads to cyclic majorities and prevents the ranking of the alternatives.

We shall now put forth a new axiomatic system leading to some satisfying solutions for this problem. Let us recall to the reader that, in order to separate the concept from other multicriterion problems, we shall speak of the multicriterion outranking problem (respectively: axioms, methods, algorithms). From Arrow's axiomatic system, we shall keep

Axiom I (Diversity)
Each criterion is a total order on a finite set X of alternatives, and there is no restriction condition on the criteria that can be any total order on X: the solution is defined everywhere. From any set of data the method has to point out orders (if necessary, the number of criteria, $|E|$, can be supposed odd).

We then need an axiom of symmetry, of normalization, which looks like May's axiom and makes precise the ordinal limitation fixed to the data:

Axiom II (Symmetry)
All the objects and all the criteria are treated equally, but as the criteria are supposed to possess noncomparable scales, the only information they provide is the existence of the pairwise preferences that they contain.

An axiom of positive responsiveness is highly desirable for an industrial decision. Many formulas yield comparable results. We propose the one which is the simplest for further proofs:

Axiom III (Positive responsiveness)
The intensity of the preference between the two alternatives x_i and x_j is a strictly increasing function of the number of criteria that rank x_i before x_j.

Let a_{ij} denote the number of criteria ranking x_i before x_j in the profile E. The matrix $A = [a_{ij}]$ will be called the *outranking matrix* associated with the profile E, and its coefficients the *outranking coefficients*. As it is the simplest cardinal utility function representing the intensity of pairwise preferences, it is the one we shall use, unless otherwise indicated. This is in fact nothing more than the model we used until now as being a paradigm for the more sophisticated ones. We thought that most of their properties were already readable—and more easily readable—on this very simple and tractable model.

The outranking matrices have a nice property that we shall call the "constant sum" property: there exists a number N (here, $N = |E|$) such that, for any (i,j), $a_{ij} + a_{ji} = N$. In other words, $[N - a_{ij}] = [a_{ij}]^t$. This property has proved to be of great heuristic value even if the corresponding assumptions have to be somehow relaxed in the sophisticated cases. The "constant sum" property can, of course, be held by matrices that are not outranking matrices.

7   Outranking Axioms

The derivation of algorithmic methods of multicriterion ranking suitable for industrial problems (henceforth called outranking methods for the sake of simplification) then needs additional axioms. They make up the material of this chapter. Its organization consists of two distinct parts. The first one deals with the sequential independence axioms, while the second will present the köhlerian axioms.

7.1   The Sequential Independence Axioms

A choice function is, as defined by Fishburn [1973], a method that allows the distinction, from among the elements of a possibly large set, of a subset of best objects, or, in the more favorable case, of the best object. The building of a multicriterion outranking can consist of the successive applications of this choice function to the subprofiles generated by each successive partition.

In other words, at step p of the algorithm, we own p already ranked equivalence classes of alternatives; we want to increase the discriminating power of this hierarchy. Step p will consist of the application of the considered choice function to one of the classes of still equivalent alternatives; but the information taken into account for the application of the choice function will be contained in the restriction of the outranking matrix to the outranking coefficients corresponding to the pairwise preferences between these alternatives. This only describes the "type" of independence required.

Sequential Independence Principle

1. The ranking is obtained through a step-by-step process, each step consisting of the partition of one class of still equivalent alternatives into a nonempty set of dominating, and a nonempty set of subjugated alternatives inside the class.

2. At each step, the relevant data are contained in the restriction of the given profile to only the subset of alternatives that will be partitioned.

Three types of such current processes then come to mind. Suppose that, for a class of considered profiles, such a choice function would always be able to point out a unique best alternative (in case of a tie, the choice could otherwise be made arbitrarily, leading to as many ties in the solution) from among the elements of any set of alternatives. A committee that has to rank candidates often likes, especially if that decision is made without dispute, to exhibit the best candidate first, then to take care of the followers, by comparison among them, and so on. This type of ranking, by sucessive identification of the best one from the remaining alternatives, will be called *decreasing ranking*. A very similar procedure, called *increasing ranking*, would begin by the elimination of the worst alternative, then proceed with the elimination of the worst from the remaining alternatives, and so on.

The mathematician can object to such a progressive outranking algorithm: the further the algorithm proceeds, the more serious will be the risk of error in the ranking by progressive impoverishment of the available information.

In our models, the argument is supposed noneffective: suppose that the decision maker turns into realities only the alternatives within the p best ranks (or needs only to eliminate the p worst candidates), this being due to budget or human constraints. As the alternatives after (respectively, prior to) the pth are discarded anyway, our theoretical decision maker does not care much for the knowledge of their exact relative rankings. In our axiomatic system, his first concern is supposed to be a rule such that a change in the ranking of the p best (respectively, worst) alternatives does not imply any change in the ranking of the remaining ones; if the information about the already chosen alternatives change for external reasons, it can be considered desirable that the next alternative to be selected relies only on the restriction of the profile to the remaining ones.

In the case where another axiom makes precise another type of sequence of dichotomous partitions leading to the expected order, the argument will of course be of another nature and is discussed more deeply in an example of the next section.

The first three axioms suppose that all the available information is contained in the outranking matrix. Then, at step p, any sequentially independent outranking method will apply to an ordered set of equivalence classes of alternatives. Hence, it will always be possible to formalize the method through the definition of a numerical function, defined on the set of the new possible partitions and called the *evaluation function*. In order to compute this function we shall need only a subset, called the *evaluation set*, of the coefficients (of the restriction of the outranking matrix to the set of alternatives on which the new partition will be made).

The first question that arises is, of course: Are there "natural" evaluation sets? The process of ranking alternatives can be considered from two opposite points of view:

dominance and subjugation. With our data, the dominance of the alternative x_p over the others is summarized by the coefficients of the pth row of the outranking matrix, and the subjugation of the same alternative, by the coefficients of the pth column. It is clear that the evaluations of two different partitions are not in general independent, even if they concern disjoint sets of alternatives. Since the evaluation sets in some well known aggregation methods are identical to the whole set of the coefficients of the matrix, changing the coefficients of one evaluation set can very well affect the coefficients of another one!

The practice of decision-making validates three different axioms of sequential independence:

Axiom IV.I (Decreasing sequential independence)

1. The ranking is obtained through a step-by-step process, each step consisting in the identification of a best element from among the not yet ranked alternatives, these being considered as subjugated by all the previously selected ones.

2. At each step, the relevant data for the identification of the best element are contained in the restriction of the given profile to only the subset of alternatives not yet ranked at that step.

Axiom IV.II (Increasing sequential independence)

1. The ranking is obtained through a step-by-step process, each step consisting in the identification of a worst element from among the not yet ranked alternatives, these being considered as dominating all the previously selected ones.

2. At each step, the relevant data are contained in the restriction of the given profile to only the subset of alternatives not yet ranked at that step.

Axiom IV.III (Dichotomous sequential independence)

1. The ranking is obtained through a step-by-step process, each step consisting in the bipartition of one class of still equivalent alternatives into a set of dominating, and a set of subjugated alternatives, all the alternatives of the first set being henceforth considered as dominating the alternatives of the second set.

2. At each step, the relevant data are contained in the restriction of the given profile to only the class of alternatives to be dichotomized at that step.

These axioms have straightforward consequences. Consider any outranking method satisfying axioms I, II, III, and IV.I (decreasing sequential independence). Suppose that the first alternative selected by the method is x_1. Because of axioms II and III, all the information is contained in the outranking matrix. Because of axiom II (symmetry), any other profile where the alternatives would be the same up to a permutation of $\{x_2, \ldots, x_n\}$, would leave x_1 as the first selected alternative. How do these permutations affect the outranking matrix? It is simple: Along the first row as along the first column, the coefficients are merely permuted according to the permutation on $\{x_2, \ldots, x_n\}$. Inside what remains of the outranking matrix after deletion of the first row and the first column, that is to say, inside the current outranking matrix for the next step of the algorithm, all the coefficients are determined by the *relative* positions along the criteria of $x_2, \ldots, x_n$, and as these, because of the symmetry axiom, should have no influence on the selection of x_1, the evaluation function of the partition that selects x_1 is seen to be only a function of row 1 and column 1. In addition, because of the "constant sum" property, such a function can be considered as a function of the coefficients in the row or in the column only. This gives the content of the following useful property:

Lemma 7.1
For an outranking method that follows axioms I–IV.I (respectively IV.II), at each current step, the evaluation function of the partition that selects the best (respectively, the worst) alternative is a symmetric function of the coefficients of the row (or the column) corresponding to the alternative in the current outranking matrix.

The equivalent property for axiom IV.III is of course less clear. Similar considerations are, as far as we know, presently being investigated by B. Debord, in the Applied Mathematics Department at the University of Grenoble. Our particular interest for the outranking methods obeying axioms IV.I and IV.II clearly comes from their similarity with some sort of logical industrial behavior: If one has a few best alternatives to select from among the elements of a large set, it will be natural to use a method of pure compared dominance (hence where the evaluation sets will be the rows of the current outranking matrix), which keeps the greatest information for the selection of the best elements; conversely, if one has a few worst alternatives to eliminate from among the elements of a large set, it will be natural as well to use a method of pure compared subjugation (hence the evaluation set will be the columns of the current outranking matrix).

The three different versions of the first four axioms discard many current methods.

Theorem 7.1
Any of the three different versions of the first four axioms discard Borda's method.

Proof Let us remind the reader that Borda's method [1781] is equivalent to using the sum of the ranks of the alternatives as a cardinal utility function on X. It has been recently identified as the only solution to axiomatic systems related to committee decision-making. See, for instance, Young [1974, 1975], and Smith [1973]. Consider the profile on $X = \{a, b, c, d\}$ composed of the following five orders: $abcd$, $bcda$, $cdab$, $dabc$, $dcba$. The outranking matrix is

```
.  3  2  1
2  .  3  2
3  2  .  3
4  3  2  .
```

Applying Borda's method to this example gives the unique solution $dcba$. Suppose now that with the version of the axioms containing axiom IV.I (decreasing sequential independence), the successive selections of the first two objects d and c would have been the same. The outranking matrix then indicates that three criteria against two prefer a to b. Hence, the sequential version would yield $dcab$.

A similar argument can be followed for the axiomatic system containing axiom IV.II (increasing sequential independence): once b and a are rejected, only c and d remain to be ranked; but the outranking matrix indicates that three criteria against two prefer c to d.

With the third system of axioms, one necessarily reaches a step where one shall have to rank, independently from the already ranked objects, one of the pairs $\{d,c\}$, or $\{a,b\}$, or $\{c,b\}$. The two first cases have already been shown to exhibit an impossibility; but the same occurs with the last pair, as three criteria against two prefer b to c.

7.2 The Köhlerian Axioms

Many of the properties we are now going to deal with can be found under a less explicit form in Köhler's thesis [1978]. We use these results in order to obtain axioms more precise than that of being Condorcet. We specified in the introduction of this chapter that, when the majority method yields intransitivities, we need a result "not too far" from a reasonable compromise. We know that the majority method will not apply to our data in general. Somewhat similar results are discussed by Kramer [1977]. His primary interest was in the equilibrium of political processes and was therefore descriptive in nature, but he also drew some implications for social choice theory (pp. 326–329). His proposal was what will be denoted as $R_{\beta+1}$. The context is different, since Kramer assumes that the alternatives form a multidimensional continuum and that each individual's preference decreases as the distance from that individual's ideal alternative to the given alternative increases.

G. Köhler had the intuition of the "köhlerian" methods while he was working on his master's thesis, which was presented orally as early as 1976. At that time, he was interested in an often investigated subject (see, for instance, Craven [1971] and Ferejohn and Grether [1974]), the "α-majorities." This expression denotes the binary relations R_α obtained on a profile on X by selection of the pairs (x_i, x_j) of alternatives such that α criteria at least agree to rank x_i better than x_j. Hence α and the outranking coefficients were integers, and N was odd. Before the mention of any special restriction, the properties that follow apply to any square nonnegative matrix $A = [a_{ij}]$ with integer coefficients and verifying the "constant sum" property for a certain N (in short, we shall speak of constant-sum matrices); α can be any real positive number, and the relation R_α contains (x_i, x_j) if and only if $a_{ij} \geqslant \alpha$.

When α is equal to zero, R_α is symmetric and complete; when α is small enough, R_α necessarily contains a total order. If A is a matrix associated with a unanimous profile, i.e., if all the criteria agree on the same total order O, R_α is equal to this same total order for any α. For any disputed profile, there exists an α small enough (for instance 1) such that R_α contains all the orders expressed by each of the criteria. Köhler was interested in $\bar{\alpha}$, the largest α such that R_α still contains a total order. We know that if $|X|$ and $|E|$ increase, the probability for $R_{|E|/2}$ to contain a total order decreases toward zero, as $R_{|E|/2}$ very probably contains a cycle and is complete. This is why the probability for $\bar{\alpha}$ to be smaller than $|E|/2$ tends to one under the same conditions.

Let us now consider $R_{\beta+1}$. For $\beta = N$, $R_{\beta+1}$ is empty, hence without cycle. When β decreases from N toward 0, $R_{\beta+1}$ begins by being cycle-free; then, for some $\underline{\beta}$, $R_{\underline{\beta}+1}$ will be the last of the sequence to be cycle-free, $R_{\underline{\beta}-p}$, $p \geqslant 0$, containing at least one cycle. If now A is obtained from N total orders on X, and if the majority method yields no intransitivity, $\underline{\beta}$ is smaller than $\bar{\alpha}$. In effect, as $R_{|E|/2}$ is cycle-free, but not $R_{\underline{\beta}}$, $\underline{\beta}$ is clearly equal to the largest a_{ij} smaller than $|E|/2$. Similarly, as $R_{|E|/2}$ contains a total order that is supposed precisely equal to $R_{\bar{\alpha}}$, and $R_{\bar{\alpha}+1}$ is no longer a complete relation, $\bar{\alpha}$ is equal to the smallest a_{ij} larger than $|E|/2$. Hence $\underline{\beta}$ is smaller than $\bar{\alpha}$.

But we know that with a large number of alternatives and criteria, this case will statistically never happen. This is why it is practical to think that, in what follows, $\bar{\alpha}$ will always be smaller than $\underline{\beta}$, $R_{\bar{\alpha}}$ will always be supposed to contain a total order, and $R_{\underline{\beta}+1}$ will be supposed cycle-free. We are now going to see that the two relations $R_{\bar{\alpha}}$ and $R_{\underline{\beta}+1}$ are very closely related.

Theorem 7.2 (Köhler [1978])
If α and β denote positive real numbers, and if $\alpha + \beta = N$, then R_α contains a total order if and only if $R_{\beta+1}$ has no cycle.

Proof

(1) $(j,i) \notin R_{\beta+1} \Leftrightarrow (i,j) \in R_\alpha$. If $(j,i) \notin R_{\beta+1}$, $a_{ij} < \beta + 1$.
Then, as $a_{ij} = N - a_{ij}$, $a_{ij} > \alpha - 1$. Hence $a_{ij} \geqslant \alpha$, and $(i,j) \in R_\alpha$. Conversely, if $(i,j) \in R_\alpha$, then $a_{ji} = N - a_{ij}$, $a_{ji} \leqslant N - \alpha = \beta$, and $a_{ji} < \beta + 1$; hence $(j,i) \notin R_{\beta+1}$.

(2) If $R_{\beta+1}$ contains no cycle, let us consider any total order O extending $R_{\beta+1}$. If $(i,j) \in O$ is not in $R_{\beta+1}$, (j,i) cannot be in $R_{\beta+1}$; otherwise O would contain a cycle. As $R_{\beta+1}$ is cycle-free, if (i,j) is in $R_{\beta+1}$, (j,i) cannot be in $R_{\beta+1}$. Hence, if $(j,i) \in O$, (j,i) is not in $R_{\beta+1}$ and $(i,j) \in R_\alpha$: all the cycle-free orders containing $R_{\beta+1}$ are contained in R_α.

(3) Let x_1 be the first alternative in a total order O included in R_α, if there is any. This means, from (1), that no object is its predecessor in $R_{\beta+1}$. Let x_2 be the second object in O. No object but x_1 can be its predecessor in $R_{\beta+1}$, and so on. Then, necessarily, $R_{\beta+1}$ has no cycle.

Theorem 7.3 (Köhler [1978])
If $\bar\alpha$ is the maximal threshold for which R_α contains a total order and $\underline\beta$ is the minimal threshold for which $R_{\beta+1}$ contains no cycle, then $\bar\alpha + \underline\beta = N$.

Proof When α increases from 0 to $\bar\alpha$, $\beta = N - \underline\alpha$ is, from the previous theorem, a threshold such that $R_{\beta+1}$ contains no cycle. When β decreases from N to $\underline\beta$, $\alpha = N - \underline\beta$ is such that R_α contains a total order. Hence $N - \alpha \leqslant \underline\beta$ and $N - \beta \geqslant \bar\alpha$. As this is true until the limit, $N - \bar\alpha \leqslant \underline\beta$, and $N - \underline\beta \geqslant \bar\alpha$, which yields $N = \bar\alpha + \underline\beta$.

Our theoretical decision maker will be a reserved man. He will be interested in the least vulnerable outranking possible. Reasonable measures of this vulnerability could be of various types, but it makes sense to imagine the most frequent styles of attack by those dissatisfied with a multicriterion ranking. In an industrial context, if anybody wants to discredit the outranking, he will look at those points in the ranking vulnerable to "legitimate" criticism, points on which this detractor would be supported by the largest majority of opponents. The two following types of weakest points cannot be denied:

1. The pairwise preferences that are obtained with a high majority and without voting paradox: Discarding these would make manifest the opposition with a large majority of criteria on a question of preferences where they will not be divided. As long as the decision maker wants to keep in his hierarchy the soundest part of the noncyclical information on the preferences he possesses, it is clear that his multicriterion ranking should include $R_{\underline{\beta}+1}$.

2. The pairwise preferences with the smallest weight in the multicriterion outranking: Consider any ranking O not contained in $R_{\bar{\alpha}}$. It contains at least a pair (x_s, x_t) that is not contained in $R_{\bar{\alpha}}$, and a_{st} is strictly smaller than $\bar{\alpha}$. In case of an attack concerning these pairs, the best defense for the decision maker would be to prove that any other total order would do worse. In other words, the multicriterion ranking, once done, yields an order O. This order, being on a finite set, contains at least one pair (x_i, x_j) such that $\underline{a}_{ij} = \min a_{ij}$ when (x_i, x_j) is element of O. The orders where $\underline{a}_{ij}$ is as large as possible are precisely the orders contained in $R_{\bar{\alpha}}$.

A surprising "constant sum" result is verified, in the case of constant sum matrices, by the total orders containing $R_{\underline{\beta}}$:

Theorem 7.4
If the outranking matrix verifies the constant sum property, then, as any O containing $R_{\underline{\beta}+1}$ is contained in $R_{\bar{\alpha}}$, any O contained in $R_{\bar{\alpha}}$ contains $R_{\underline{\beta}+1}$.

Proof The first part of the result has just been established. We proved an even stronger result in the proof of theorem 7.3. Any cycle-free binary relation containing $R_{\underline{\beta}+1}$ is contained in $R_{\bar{\alpha}}$, and O is just a special case of a cycle-free binary relation. In order to prove the second part of the theorem, let us consider $(x_p, x_q) \in R_{\underline{\beta}+1}$, and let O be any ordering included in $R_{\bar{\alpha}}$. Suppose that $(x_p, x_q) \notin O$. Then, as O is a total order, (x_q, x_p) would be in O. Hence $a_{qp} \geq \bar{\alpha}$. As a_{pq} was supposed strictly larger than $\underline{\beta}$, $a_{pq} + a_{qp} > \bar{\alpha} + \underline{\beta}$. But because of the "constant sum" property, $a_{pq} + a_{qp} = |E| = \bar{\alpha} + \underline{\beta}$. This equality contradicts the former inequality. In the "constant sum" case, then, for a total order, containing $R_{\underline{\beta}+1}$ or being contained in $R_{\bar{\alpha}}$ are equivalent properties.

In general, we shall say

Definition 7.1
An order O extending $R_{\underline{\beta}+1}$ is bold on a sound but narrow background.

Definition 7.2
An order O contained in $R_{\bar{\alpha}}$ is cautious on a weak but broad background.

Definition 7.3
If the constant sum property holds, we shall say that O is a prudent outranking if it contains $R_{\underline{\beta}+1}$ and is contained in $R_{\bar{\alpha}}$.

Once again, if the constant sum property holds, the synthesis is not contradictory. This is why it would be more than reasonable in our industrial case to propose this axiom:

Axiom V' (Prudence)
The solution of the outranking method must be a prudent order.

Weaker axioms of a similar form can of course be obtained using the condition with $R_{\bar{\alpha}}$ or $R_{\beta+1}$ only. It must be remarked that, though he did not see the connection with $R_{\bar{\alpha}}$ in his paper, Kramer [1977] saw the very strong interest, from a purely theoretical axiomatic point of view, of the relation $R_{\beta+1}$ itself. If one does not need a total relation, which is not the case in our industrial context, the function that aggregates a profile into the partial relation $R_{\beta+1}$ can be a satisfactory aggregation function, axiomatically characterized by a reasonable relaxation of Arrow's axioms.

Let us now remind the reader that Kemeny's method, extensively presented in Kemeny and Snell [1960], was proposed as a solution to the problem of finding a consensus preference order for alternatives being considered by a group of experts. It then appeared as the solution of the minimization of a sum of squares of distances between orders. This minimization is equivalent to the maximization of the sum of the outranking coefficients corresponding to the ordered pairs in the order. Levenglick and Young [1978] proved that this method is the only one to be Condorcet and "consistent." The choice function D is consistent if, E and E' being two profiles on X such that $D(E)$ $\cap$ $D(E') \neq \emptyset$, then $D(E + E') \cap D(E) \cap D(E')$. This "consistency," which makes sense in political issues, did not seem to us efficiently interpretable for industrial situations, that is, as a "business-like" criterion.

The straightforward translation of this axiom in terms of industrial practice seems to be as follows: two disjoint sets of experts evaluate the same set of alternatives. The application of the common choice function leads, respectively, to a choice set D and to a choice set D'. Then the axiom asks that the procedure applied to the individual evaluations put together yield a choice set contained in $D \cap D'$. The "consistency" criterion has definite ethical content and is therefore relevant to welfare economics and political science. But here our aim is operations research, of use to businessmen. We are unable to see why the "consistency" criterion has any compelling justification when efficiency is the prime consideration.

There is, in fact, a deep criticism of Kemeny's solution from the point of view of a conflict averse decision maker:

Theorem 7.5
Axiom V' discards Kemeny's method.

This is easy to prove by the exhibition of a counterexample (used by Köhler in his dissertation for another proof). $X = \{1,2,3,4,5\}$, and the profile contains the following orders: 33 criteria indicate 5 2 3 4 1, 19 criteria indicate 1 5 2 3 4; 18 criteria indicate 4 1 2 3 5, 10 criteria indicate 4 1 3 5 2; 10 criteria indicate 1 3 4 5 2, 10 criteria indicate 3 4 2 1 5. This profile yields the outranking matrix:

XX	57	57	29	67
43	XX	70	52	28
43	30	XX	72	48
71	48	28	XX	48
33	72	52	52	XX

It is easy to compute both Kemeny's solution and a prudent order. Kemeny's solution, 41523, yields a total of 570 for the sum of its corresponding outranking coefficients. But it contains the preference "4 better than 3," on which only 28 ballots agree. On the contrary, the weakest preference of 52341, which is the unique prudent order, is "5 better than 1" with 33 ballots (but the sum of its outranking coefficients is only 560).

Axiom V' can be justified in fact by another property of the prudent orders that deserves attention (conjectured by M. Ayel, oral communication, 1982). Imagine that our theoretical decision maker wishes to be a prompter, a democratic leader, rather than a boss. He is not the one who produces; he is the one who helps the others produce. When he has to make a difficult decision of ranking, he gathers his specialists and discusses the pros and cons with them, and the scales oscillate. Very often the scales do not stop oscillating, due to cyclic majorities.

Then the decision maker has to impose a more or less disputable hierarchy. As he is a "democrat," he will be willing to use his power in such a way as to introduce into the set of individual opinions the smallest possible distortion. Using our model, he constitutes, from the profile E (supposed normalized) of the rankings of his specialists, a new profile $E + wO$, which is obtained from E by adding w criteria identical to his personal ranking.

If he applies the majority method of decision with w large enough, he will act as a dictator. If, on the contrary, he takes a too small w, the majority decision rule will not apply. But there exists a smallest w such that the majority method, applied to the profile E completed by w identical criteria, gives a cycle-free solution. More generally, let O be a total order on X. Let E be a normalized profile with $|E| = N$, and $E + wO$ the profile obtained by the adjunction to E of w criteria identical to O.

Theorem 7.5

If $M(\Pi)$ denotes the result of the application of the majority method to the arbitrary profile Π, if E denotes a profile such that $M(E)$ contains intransitivities, if we assume that w is even and N odd, so that the number of criteria in the profile remains odd after the addition of the w criteria to the profile E:

(a) If $M(E + wO)$ is cycle-free, then $w \geqslant \underline{w} = \underline{\beta} - \bar{\alpha} + 1$.

(b) For any O, $M(E + \underline{w}O)$ is included in $R_{\bar{\alpha}}$.

(c) If O is included in $R_{\bar{\alpha}}$, $M(E + \underline{w}O) = O$.

Proof

(a) If $w < \underline{\beta} - \bar{\alpha} + 1$, and is even, then, for any O, $M(E + wO)$ contains cycles. Indeed, since $N = \bar{\alpha} + \underline{\beta}$ and is odd, $\underline{\beta} - \bar{\alpha} + 1$ is clearly an even number. $N + w$ is smaller than $2\underline{\beta} + 1$, so that $\underline{\beta}$ criteria constitute a majority in the profile $E + wO$. But, by definition, $R_{\underline{\beta}}$ contains a cycle, and this cycle will be equally contained in $M(E + wO)$.

(b) If $w = \underline{w}$, as $N + \underline{w} = 2\underline{\beta} + 1$, the majority in $E + \underline{w}O$ requires at least $\underline{\beta} + 1$ criteria. Therefore $(x_p, x_q) \in M(E + \underline{w}O)$ implies, if $(x_p, x_q) \in O$, that $a_{pq} + \underline{w} > \underline{\beta} + 1$, and $a_{pq} \geqslant \underline{\beta} + 1$ otherwise. In both cases, $a_{pq} + \underline{w} > \underline{\beta} + 1$. From the definition of $\underline{w}$ it follows that $a_{pq} \geqslant \bar{\alpha}$, so that $(x_p, x_q) \in R_{\bar{\alpha}}$.

(c) Suppose that O is an order included in $R_{\bar{\alpha}}$ and that $(x_p, x_q) \in O$. Then, in $E + \underline{w}O$, $a_{pq} + \underline{w}$ criteria rank x_p before x_q. The fact that $a_{pq} \geqslant \bar{\alpha}$ and $\underline{w} = \underline{\beta} - \bar{\alpha} + 1$ imply that at least $\underline{\beta} + 1$ criteria prefer x_p over x_q, so that $(x_p, x_q) \in M(E + \underline{w}O)$. Thus, O is included in $M(E + \underline{w}O)$. As it is irreflexive and complete, $M(E + \underline{w}O)$ cannot be strictly larger and $O = M(E + \underline{w}O)$.

It can be shown that $M(E + \underline{w}O)$ may be cycle-free even if O is not included in $R_{\bar{\alpha}}$, but $M(E + \underline{w}O)$ will not be O but rather be some order included in R_α. As an example, one can consider the profile $E = abc, abc, bca, bca, cab$. It yields $\underline{\beta} = 3$; $\bar{\alpha} = 2$ and therefore $\underline{w} = 2$. There are at least two criteria for any alternative against any other, except for cb. Hence, R_2 contains all orderings for which b is prefered to c, i.e., abc, bac, and bca. Consider then acb, which is not included in R_2. Straightforward calculations show that $M(E + 2acb) = abc$, which is an ordering included in R_2.

This spirit of prudence, in order to lead toward determinate solutions, must be followed to its ultimate logical consequences. In the majority of real situations, the available choice function will not select a unique best alternative, but will rather point out a partition between two sets, of comparable sizes: the set of the "good" ones, and the set of the "bad" ones. At that point, if we suppose that the whole ranking process has to be defended in front of a board of directors, what is the point on which the decision maker can be the most vulnerable? Clearly once again, he is "legitimately" vulnerable if he presents a dichotomy in which alternative x belongs to the dominating class, alternative y belongs to the dominated class, and the proportion of criteria preferring y to x is very high! In the case where the pairwise preferences of any object of the first class over any object of the second is expressed by a majority of criteria, it will be natural to say that the partition is "Condorcet."

The reasonable axiom to introduce now should be in the line of the generalizations of being "Condorcet" we already proposed for the rankings. This axiom must demand that each one of the partitions made in sequence, as well as the final result, should be "as prudent as possible." Of course, the independence axiom should be respected: the restriction of the profile to the alternatives in a set Y should be the only information taken into account, if the algorithm must select a partition for Y.

One can naturally define "prudence for a partition" in the following way: Let E be a set bipartitioned into a subset E' of dominant alternatives, and a subset E'' of subjugated alternatives. Let $a(E',E'')$ be the smallest of the outranking coefficients of all the pairs of alternatives made with its first alternative in E' and the second in E''.

Definition 7.4

A bipartition of a set E into a subset E' of dominant and a subset E'' of subjugated alternatives will be "prudent" if, for any possible such bipartitions of E into F' and F'', $a(F',F'') \leq a(E',E'')$.

It is now possible to formulate the axiom of prudence under its ultimate logical form:

Axiom V (Sequential prudence)

A sequential outranking process will be sequentially prudent if:

each step is a prudent bipartition,

and the result is a prudent order.

Let us describe its practical meaning for the cases that obey axiom IV.I or IV.II. Suppose, for instance, the alternatives are ranked from the best to the worst. At each step of the ranking process, ranking the next alternative is not different from determinating a partition of the set of the not yet ranked (and thus "worse") alternatives, with the constraint that the dominant subset contain only one alternative. Suppose now that the decision maker is presenting a ranking in front of a board of directors and that the pth object is the first one in the sequence to be disputed. It will be necessarily disputed on the "weakest" of the preferences it implies. However, if this new partition is such that any other partition would be worse, the decision maker has the best argument: any other choice would be more scandalous!

It remains for the last chapter to identify practical methods satisfying the axioms.

8   Outranking Methods

This chapter leaves open many questions that may be considered as incentives for the researcher: the axioms presented in chapter 7 can be modified and combined in different ways, leading to a whole field of solutions allowing considerable freedom to model various behaviors and solve different problems. Unless otherwise mentioned, the profiles are still composed of total orders. The notation for the outranking matrices stays the same. $A = [a_{ij}]$ is the outranking matrix corresponding to the profile E.

After two general remarks on the properties of the three systems of axioms (having in common axioms I, II, III, and V), we shall completely identify the outranking methods characterized by the first systems of axioms and give indications about the other problems.

8.1 General Remarks

Theorem 8.1
The majority method, when its application is limited to the profiles that do not lead to any intransitivity, satisfies any of the three systems of axioms.

Proof Let us consider the first axiomatic system; the first selected alternative according to this system is necessarily the Condorcet winner. Because of the constant sum property, any other choice would introduce within the final order an outranking coefficient smaller than the majority, which would not satisfy axiom V. The second selected alternative is the Condorcet winner from among the remaining alternatives, etc. The same reasoning can be applied to the second system as well. For the third system, it is easy to understand that, for any partition coherent with the majority ranking, all the outranking coefficients will be larger than the majority, and that any of the other partitions would contain at least one pair with a coefficient smaller than the majority. It is clear that, as long as they respect the majority ranking, the successive partitions will eventually reach the majority ranking.

There remains to observe that this majority order is the only prudent order corresponding to such a profile: all its outranking coefficients are larger than the majority, and any other order would have at least one coefficient smaller than this majority.

Theorem 8.2
The evaluation functions of the successive partitions made through the algorithmic process cannot be the sum of the outranking coefficients.

Proof   Use the first system of axioms, the choice of the first element in the example in chapter 7; theorem 7.5 would give 1 as the first alternative, when the unique prudent order begins by 5. With the second system of axioms, the last objects could be equally 2 or 3, when 1 is the only possible solution! Finally, with the third system, the sum of the coefficients corresponding to the dichotomy $\{1,4\}$, $\{2,3,5\}$ reaches a total of 305, while $\{5,2\}$, $\{3,1,4\}$, the "best" among the dichotomies respecting the only prudent solution, gives 302. This proves that the unique prudent order could not be reached sequentially if the evaluation function was the sum of the outranking coefficients associated with the selected partition.

8.2 Köhler's Method

The first system of axioms leaves a very limited choice for the algorithm, namely, the solution imagined by Köhler essentially as a speedy way to obtain $\bar{\alpha}$:

Algorithm 8.1 (Köhler's primal algorithm [1978])
Step r: Identify the minimum a_{ij} along each row of the current matrix. One at least from among these minima is larger than the others. If there are ties, one from among them is chosen arbitrarily. The row of this minimum corresponds to an alternative that will be ranked at the rth rank in the multicriterion ranking. If $r < n$, delete the corresponding row and column of the outranking matrix in order to obtain the current outranking matrix for the $(r + 1)$th step. The algorithm stops when the outranking matrix becomes empty.

It is remarkable that this greedy algorithm, a sequence of local prudent decisions, leads in turn to a global prudent result!

Theorem 8.3 (Köhler [1978])
Even if the constant sum properly does not hold, even if the solution is not unique, Köhler's algorithm yields a ranking contained in $R_{\bar{\alpha}}$, and the minimum of the successive maxima is equal to $\bar{\alpha}$.

Proof Using Köhler's algorithm on the outranking matrix A gives at least one ranking O. The minimum of the maxima of the minima of the coefficients of the rows of the successive matrices corresponds to at least one pair (r,s) of indices such that $a_{rs} = \min_{(k,l)\in O} a_{kl}$. Let O' be another order with $b = \min_{(i,j)\in O'} a_{ij}$. Let Y be the set of the followers of x_r in O. If x_r is, in O', before the elements of Y, it implies, as x_s is in Y, that $(x_r,x_s) \in O'$. Hence b will be smaller than or equal to a_{rs}.

If x_r is not ranked, in O', before all the elements of Y, it is ranked after y, the element of Y being the first in O' from among the elements of $Y + x_r$. Let now $O'(Y + x_r)$ denote the restriction of O' to the elements of $Y + z_r$;

$$b = \min_{(i,j)\in O'} a_{ij} \leq \min_{(i,j)\in O'(x + Y_r)} a_{ij},$$

which is in its turn smaller than or equal to $\min a_{ij}$ in the row corresponding to y in the submatrix restricted to the alternatives in $Y + x_r$ because, while it was applied to the same submatrix, the algorithm selected another row. Accordingly, this last minimum was smaller than or equal to a_{rs}, which is thus equal to $\bar{\alpha}$.

It is clear that a dual algorithm, acting on the columns, can be described:

Algorithm 8.2 (Köhler's dual algorithm)
Step r: Identify the maximum a_{ij} along each column of the current outranking matrix. One at least of these maxima is smaller than the others. In case of ties, one from among them is chosen arbitrarily. The column of this maximum corresponds to an alternative that will be ranked at the rth rank in the multicriterion ordering. Proceed as in algorithm 8.1, and the process will stop when the outranking matrix becomes void.

Theorem 8.4
Even if the constant sum property does not hold, even if the solution is not unique, Köhler's dual algorithm yields a

ranking contained in $R_{\beta+1}$ and the maximum of the successive minima is equal to $\underline{\beta}$.

Hint: If a set of pairwise preferences is cycle-free, it is contained in a total order. Finding the largest $R_{\beta+1}$ is of course equivalent to finding $R_{\beta+1}$. If one finds an order O such that, under the main diagonal, the largest coefficient is the smallest possible when O varies, then all the pairs with a larger outranking coefficient will be elements of $R_{\beta+1}$. No additional ones could be; otherwise the outranking relation would contain at least one cycle.

Without any special difficulty, the reader will obtain through similar proofs similar results for the algorithms working by progressive elimination.

8.3 Arrow-Raynaud's Method

The second system of axioms allows only a limited possibility for the algorithm as well:

Algorithm 8.3 (Arrow-Raynaud's primal algorithm)
Step r: Identify the *maximum* a_{ij} along each row of the current matrix. One at least from among these maxima is smaller than the others. If there are ties, one from among them is chosen arbitrarily. The row of this minimum corresponds to an alternative that will be ranked at the $(n - r + 1)$th rank in the multicriterion ranking. If $r < n$, delete the corresponding row and column of the outranking matrix, in order to obtain the current outranking matrix for the $(r + 1)$th step. The algorithm stops when the outranking matrix becomes void.

Theorem 8.5
Even if the constant sum property does not hold, even if the solution is not unique, Arrow-Raynaud's algorithm

yields a ranking containing $R_{\underline{\beta} + 1}$, and the minimum of the successive maxima is equal to $\underline{\beta}$.

Proof   Using Arrow-Raynaud's algorithm on our outranking matrix gives at least one ranking O. The maximum of the minima of the maxima corresponds to at least one coefficient a_{sr}. Let O^+ be the reverse of O. In the outranking matrix displayed according to O, the outranking coefficients of O^+ are all under the main diagonal. It is trivial to verify that $a_{sr} = \max_{(i,j) \in O^+} a_{ij}$. This coefficient is by construction located under the main diagonal in such a way that s can be supposed larger than r. Let O' be another order with $b = \max_{(i,j) \in O'} a_{ij}$. If O contains $R_{\underline{\beta} + 1}$, that means that a_{sr} is less than or equal to $\underline{\beta}$, while it is the largest of the outranking coefficients corresponding to pairs not in $R_{\underline{\beta} + 1}$. All the other pairs will be contained in O, hence will not constitute any cycle. If, for any O', b is greater than or equal to a_{sr}, then the threshold corresponding to the cycle-free part of O will be the lowest possible, and a_{sr} will be equal to $\underline{\beta}$.

Let Y be the set of the predecessors of x_s in O. If x_s is, in O', after the elements of Y, as x_r is contained in Y, a_{sr} will remain under the main diagonal of the outranking matrix displayed according to O'. Hence b, its largest element under the main diagonal, will be greater than or equal to a_{sr}. If x_s is not ranked, in O', after the elements of Y, it is at least before y, the element of Y being the last in O' from among the elements of $Y + x_s$. Let now $O'(Y + x_s)$ denote the restriction of O' to the elements of $Y + x_s$;

$$b = \max_{(i,j)\,\in O'} a_{ij} \geq \max_{(i,j)\,\in O'\ (Y + x_s)} a_{ij},$$

itself greater than max a_{ij} in the row corresponding to y in the submatrix restricted to the alternatives in $Y + x_s$ because, while it was applied to the same submatrix, the algorithm selected another row. From this it necessarily results that this last maximum was greater than or equal to x_{sr}.

Arrow-Raynaud's and Köhler's dual algorithms are of course similar. It is clear that, with the additional constant sum hypothesis, all these results can be deduced straightforwardly from the first one. It is remarkable, however, to observe that the two different classes of algorithms can very well yield, on a constant sum matrix, different solutions for the prudent orders eventually obtained: processing through successive rejects or successive selections is effectively very different! Consider, for instance, the profile 3241, 2143, 1324, 4213, 4312, 4132, 1234. Its outranking matrix is

```
X  4  5  3
3  X  3  4
2  4  X  3
4  3  4  X
```

Each algorithm yields five solutions. Four are common solutions to both algorithms: 1234, 1324, 2413, 4132. Arrow-Raynaud's algorithm yields 4123 and not Köhler's, whereas Köhler's algorithm yields 1432 and not Arrow-Raynaud's.

Small and simple examples are difficult to find because they must imply some effective loss of information between the first and the last ranked objects, and in addition generate a reasonably wide set of prudent orders. Of course, if the constant sum property holds, Arrow-Raynaud's primal algorithm will be identical (in its results) to Köhler's dual, and Köhler's primal to Arrow-Raynaud's dual.

Through the formalization of these four algorithms appear only the axioms IV.I and IV.II. The relaxations of axiom V suggested by the variations around the theme of being not sequentially prudent, but, for instance, sequentially "bold on a sound but marrow" or "cautious on a weak but broad" background, could be treated similarly! The same techniques can directly prove that these algorithms identify $\bar{\alpha}$ and $\underline{\beta}$, and respectively lead to orders contained in $R_{\bar{\alpha}}$, or containing $R_{\underline{\beta}+1}$.

8.4 Additional Remarks

Theorem 8.6
If the prudent order is unique, only an algorithm coinciding with Köhler's algorithm will sequentially exhibit this prudent order.

Proof Suppose the unique prudent order O is identified and the outranking matrix ordered according to O. Then the first row of the outranking matrix is the only one where all the coefficients are larger than or equal to $\bar{\alpha}$, as one coefficient at least in the other rows is strictly smaller than $\bar{\alpha}$. Hence, Köhler's criterion allows the identification of the first alternative in O. The fact that the method has to be sequential proves the rest of the result.

In the field of the axiomatic systems containing axioms IV.I and IV.II, we feel that at least three interesting conjectures remain open:

In the constant sum case: Arrow-Raynaud's and Köhler's algorithms build the totality of the prudent orders.

Köhler's dual and Arrow-Raynaud are enough to build all the orders "sequentially containing $R_{\underline{\beta}+1}$," once this concept is conveniently defined.

Similarly, Köhler and Arrow-Raynaud's dual are enough to build all the orders "sequentially contained in $R_{\bar{\alpha}}$."

The aim of this book is to open new questions rather than to close old ones, and we had one hope that must unfortunately probably be dismissed! We thought for a good while that Köhler's algorithm, in the constant sum case, could be characterized by a simpler axiomatic system where the last axioms would be merely

1. The ranking is obtained through a step-by-step process, each step consisting of the ranking of a next alternative.

2. At each step, the relevant data is contained in the restriction of the given profile to only the alternatives not yet ranked.

3. The result must be a prudent order.

However "loose," this sequential independence has many important consequences: it is easy to associate an evaluation function to each of the alternatives not yet ranked, and to define the evaluation set of such a function as the set of outranking coefficients on which the evaluation function will be computed for each of the remaining alternatives.

Because of the "constant sum" property, one still can show that at each current step, the evaluation function of an alternative is a symmetric function of the coefficients of its row (or column) in the outranking matrix. This alone would justify the interest in methods of pure dominance or pure subjugation.

It is still easy to show that the notion of independence contained in these axioms discards Borda's method (consider the profile {abcd, bcda, cdab, dabc, dcba}) and Kemeny's method (consider the profile {abcd, dacb, cbda}). It is trivial to check that Kemeny's solution is unique. It is acbd, with Σa_{ij} equal to 11. This solution contains all the pairs but one of those for which the a_{ij} are equal to 2. According to the axioms, the evaluation set must be the row of the outranking matrix, which is

X   2   2   1
1   X   1   2
1   2   X   2
2   1   1   X

Rows 1 and 3 on one hand and 2 and 4 on the other hand are identical up to a permutation of their coefficients. Hence, in both cases, there should be a tie in the choice of a first element, and Kemeny's method should have given at least two solutions.

But we could not identify the whole set of methods satisfying this simpler system.

We would like to finish this chapter with the expression of another open question oriented toward efficient methods. Consider all the sequentially prudent algorithms. In some way, the evaluation function of the algorithm is a restriction of the optimization criterion for the multicriterion ranking. We want to obtain at the end an order the smallest coefficient of which is the largest possible; and in order to select the next best partition, we identify among the possible ones, the partition containing the largest possible smallest coefficient.

In any sequential outranking algorithm, one applies the evaluation function to the evaluation sets in order to determine the next selected partition. Suppose that the objective function for the outranking order is defined on the set of the outranking coefficients corresponding to the pairs in the order. If the objective function and the evaluation function could be considered as being "the same," the considered outranking method could be said to be *extensive*. We wrote "the same" within quotation marks because it is clearly not easy to speak of identical functions when they apply to sets even different in cardinality, and thus our suggestion is not very precise. We have already described in this chapter a series of methods that we could identify as "extensive." But a nice question remains open: If one replaces axiom V by the axiom *The method must be "extensive,"* it would be very interesting to see how much this condition can limit the domain of the solutions.

Annex 1: A Short Presentation of Electre I

A decision maker has to make a decision that consists of selecting the best elements out of a finite set of alternatives on which he knows the values corresponding to a finite set of criteria. More precisely, the decision maker (1) knows, for each criterion, a weak ordering (complete relation with ties) on the whole set of the alternatives, (2) must assign positive weights to all the criteria, and (3) must be able to attribute a numerical value to each step of these last scales. In other words, the decision maker must have trade-off ratios for all the criteria.

(4) The decision-maker should also decide the value of three numbers: c, d, s. The first, c, is called the "concordance threshold." Let W_{xy} be the sum of the weights of the criteria ranking x before or equal to y. Let W be the sum of the weights of all the criteria. In order to be eligible, a pairwise preference must "satisfy the concordance filter:" x better than y is an eligible preference if and only if $W_{xy}/W \geqslant c$.

The other numbers, d and s, allow the description of the discordance filter; d is a positive real number and s an integer. Consider once again the preference "x is better than y," and let us suppose that it satisfies the concordance filter. Consider the criteria that, on the contrary, ranked y at a (strictly) better rank than x. They are called the discordant criteria. The values of the distances between y and x on the scales of the discordant criteria are computed in the common arbitrary unit, and ranked from the largest to the smallest. We denote by D_{xy} the $(s + 1)$th element of this list and call it the discordance for the preference "x better than y." This preference will "satisfy the discordance filter" if and only if $D_{xy} \leq d$.

In Electre, the preferences that satisfy both filters are put together and constitute "the outranking relation." The *base* of a relation is defined as the subset of the set of alternatives that are dominated by no other element. The base of the outranking relation is the set of the elements selected by Electre.

Three criticisms can be leveled at the method: (1) The base is often empty! (2) In practice, the consultant tries different choices for the thresholds, the weights, or the trade-offs, in order to obtain a selected set as wished by the decision maker, or, sometimes, in order to obtain a nonempty base. This point is the one that contributed most to cause Electre to be discarded. (3) If one possesses the elements necessary to the building of a linear utility function, why should one try a method as sophisticated as Electre?

Annex 2: How to Recognize, If Any Exists, the Reference Orders According to Which a Given Profile Could Be Blackian?

Snakes oscillating from the top to the bottom of an Aztec pyramid was the very Mexican inspiration that suggested to Romero the solution of the problem.

What Is a Pyramid?

A pyramid is a special array of symbols from a finite set. Let us for instance consider the set $X = \{1, 2, 3, 4, 5, 6\}$. The following pyramid on X is built with 123456 as reference order:

```
          6 1
        5 1 6 2
      4 1 5 2 6 3
    3 1 4 2 5 3 6 4
  2 1 3 2 4 3 5 4 6 5
1 1 2 2 3 3 4 4 5 5 6 6
```

Following the lines according to which the same symbol is repeated will make clear the structure of the pyramid.

A pyramid on $X = \{1, 2, 3, \ldots, n\}$ would appear as follows:

				1	n							
			2	n	1	$n-1$						
		3	n	2	$n-1$	1	$n-2$					
	n	3	$n-1$	2	$n-2$	1						
	$n-3$			$n-1$	3	$n-2$	2			4		
$n-2$	n	$n-3$					2	4	1	3		
$n-1$	n	$n-2$	$n-1$	$n-3$	$n-2$			3	4	2	3	1	2
n	n	$n-1$	$n-1$	$n-2$	$n-2$	$n-3$		4	3	3	2	2	1	1

What Is a snake?

A snake is a sequence of symbols that draw a special design on the pyramid. The last element of the snake is one of the two elements at the top of the pyramid. The second last element of the snake is one of the two elements contained in one of the three positions immediately under the position of the last chosen element, but from among the two elements not already chosen. This will become clear via examples: 435261, 345216, 546321, 453216 are snakes relative to our first pyramid.

What Is the Principle of Romero's Algorithm?

It can be easily proved by induction on n that the snakes are identical to the orders following Black's condition for the reference orders that can be read at the lowest level of the pyramid, from the right to the left or from the left to the right. The principle of the algorithm, being given a set of total orders on a finite set, will be to see whether a pyramid containing them as snakes can be built up. This will be described by an example: consider the set of total orderings on X = {1, 2, 3, 4, 5, 6, 7, 8} given by 32456781, 45362718, 65432178.

In order to describe in short the possible solutions to the problem, we have to introduce the notion of pivot, which will be denoted by *, and which will be interpretable in the following way. Suppose that two pyramids can be a solution to the problem, and that the only difference between the two of them is that one is built exactly like the other seen through a mirror (what was on the left goes to the right, and conversely). The convention will consist of representing only one of the two pyramids explicitly, with a * at its top.

Then, reading the last elements of the three orders in question obliges the solution pyramid, if it exists, to be of this type:

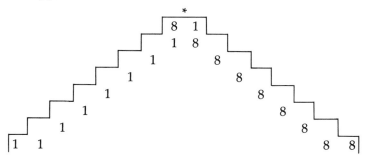

Reading the two last elements shows that a 7 must be under the top row, and this contributes to the filling up of the pyramid in the following way:

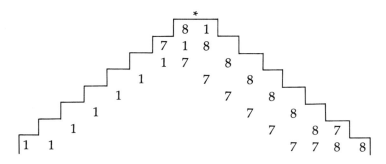

Reading the third last element of the three criteria does not bring more information, as they are compatible with the already partially designed pyramid. Reading the next elements indicates on the contrary, that elements 6 and 2 can be met without contradiction at the top of a "subpyramid," contained in the first one, but separated from it by a pivot. This will be represented naturally by the following notation.

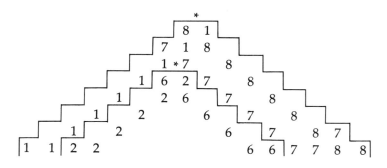

The next step in the reading of the criteria will indicate that 5's and 3's are necessarily displayed inside the small pyramid in a unique way:

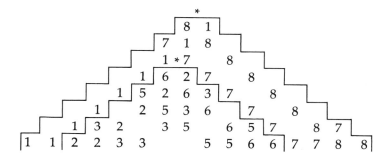

The remaining place for the 4's is unique, but it is easily checked that it is not in contradiction with the criteria:

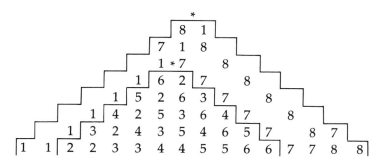

Hence, the reference orders for which the given profile can be considered as Blackian are 12345678, 87654321, 16543278, 87234561.

We have to mention that Romero's algorithm, in a much less intuitive form, can be shown to need only a single reading of the criteria. Its needs in terms of computation time grow linearly with the number of alternatives; but, as we know large Blackian profiles are very rare, the calculations, for a profile containing many different criteria, will probably reach an impossibility very soon after their beginning.

References

Abello, J. [1981] Toward a maximum consistent set. Technical Report 1-1, Department of Computer Science, University of California, Santa Barbara.

Abello, J. [1985] Intrinsic limitations of the majority rule, an algorithmic approach. *SIAM Journal on Algebraic and Discrete Methods* 6:133–144.

Arrow, K. J. [1951] *Social Choice and Individual Values.* New York: Cowles Foundation and Wiley.

Arrow, K. J. [1963] *Social Choice and Individual Values.* New Haven, Connecticut: Yale University Press, second edition.

Bernard, G., and M. L. Besson [1971] Douze méthodes d'analyse multicritère. *Revue Française d'Informatique et de Recherche Operationelle* 5:19–64.

Black, D. [1948] On the rationale of group decision-making. *Journal of Political Economy* 56:23–34.

Black, D. [1958] *The Theory of Committees and Elections.* Cambridge: Cambridge University Press.

Black, D., and R. A. Newing [1951] *Committee Decisions with Complementary Valuations.* London: William Hodge & Co.

Blin, J. M. [1973] The general concept of multidimensional consistency: some algebraic aspects of the aggregation problem. In *Multiple-Criteria Decision-Making.* Columbia, SC: University of South Carolina Press.

Borda, J. C. [1781] *Mémoire sur les Élections au Scrutin*. Paris: Mémoires de l'Académie des Sciences.

Condorcet, M. J. A. M. Caritat, Marquis de [1785] *Essai sur l'Application de l'Analyse à la Probabilitié des Décisions rendues à la pluralité des voix*. Paris: L'Imprimerie Royale.

Coombs, C. H. [1954] Social choice and strength of preference. In R. M. Thrall, C. H. Coombs, and R. L. Davis (eds.), *Decision Processes*. New York: Wiley.

Coombs, C. H. [1964] *A Theory of Data*. New York: Wiley, pp. 395–397.

Craven, J. [1971] Majority voting and social choice. *Review of Economic Studies* 38:265–267.

Duncker, K. [1903; translated in 1945] *On Problem Solving*. Washington, DC: American Psychological Association, Psychological Monographs 58, No. 5.

Dutta, B., and P. K. Pattanaik [1978] On nicely consistent voting systems. *Econometrica* 46:163–179.

Ebbinghaus, H. [1885; translated in 1964] *Memory*. New York: Wiley.

Eckenrode, R. T. [1965] Weighting multiple criteria. *Management Science* 12:180–192.

Farquharson, R. [1969] *Theory of Voting*. New Haven: Yale University Press.

Ferejohn, J., and D. Grether [1974], Rational social decision procedures. *J. Econ. Theory* 8:471–482.

Fine, B., and K. Fine [1974] Social choice and individual ranking, I and II. *Review of Economic Studies* 41:303–322, 459–475.

Fishburn, P. C. [1970] *Utility Theory for Decision Making*. New York: Wiley.

Fishburn, P. C. [1973] *The Theory of Social Choice*. Princeton, NJ: Princeton University Press.

Fishburn, P. C., W. V. Gehrlein, and E. Maskin [1979] Condorcet's proportions and Kelly's conjecture. *Discrete Applied Mathematics* 1:229–252.

Gibbard, A. [1973] Manipulation of voting schemes: a general result. *Econometrica* 41:587–601.

Gilbaud, G. Th. [1968] *Eléments de la Théorie Mathématique des Jeux*. Paris: Dunod, Monographies de Recherche Opérationnelle.

Inada, K.-I. [1964] A note on the simple majority decision rule. *Econometrica* 32:525–531.

Johnsen, E. [1968] *Studies in Multiobjective Decision Models*. Lund: Berlingska Boklryekeriet, Economic Research Center in Lund, Student Litteratur, Monograph #1.

Kemeny, J. G., and J. L. Snell [1960] *Mathematical Models in the Social Sciences*. Boston: Ginn.

Köhler, G. [1976] La prévention de l'effet Condorcet et quelques propriétés du graphe de surclassement pour les seuils 0 à 100%. Mémoire de DEA de Recherche Opérationelle, mimeo, Université Scientifique et Médicale de Grenoble.

Köhler, G. [1978] *Choix Multicritère et Analyse Algébrique des Données Ordinales*. Thesis of the 3rd Cycle, Université Scientifique et Médicale de Grenoble (France).

Kramer, G. H. [1973] On a class of equilibrium conditions for majority rule. *Econometrica* 41:285–297.

Kramer, G. H. [1976] A note on single-peakedness. *International Economic Review* 17:498–502.

Kramer, G. H. [1977] A dynamic model of political equilibrium. *Journal of Economic Theory* 16:310–334.

Levenglick, A., and H. P. Young [1978] A consistent extension of Condorcet's election principle. *SIAM Journal of Applied Mathematics* 35:285–300.

Maslow, A. H. [1954] and [1970] *Motivation and Personality*. New York: Harper & Row.

May, K. O. [1952] A set of independent necessary and sufficient conditions for simple majority decision. *Econometrica* 20:680–684.

Morton, G. [1966] Inada, Ken-ichi; a note on the simple majority decision rule. *Mathematical Reviews* 194:Review No. 1119.

Niemi, R. G., and H. F. Weisberg [1968] A mathematical solution for the probability of the paradox of voting. *Behavioral Sciences* 13:317–323.

Peleg, B. [1978] Consistent voting systems. *Econometrica* 46:153–170.

Raynaud, H. [1979] A propos de quelques conditions de transitivité de la méthode majoritaire bien connues. Colloque Aide à la Decision et Jeux de Stratégies: Aspects Multi-Critères, Bruxelles Institut des Hautes Etudes.

Raynaud, H. [1981a] Paradoxical results from Inada's conditions for majority rule. Technical Report 331, Center for Research on Organizational Efficiency, Institute for Mathematical Studies in the Social Sciences, Encina Hall, Stanford University.

Raynaud, H. [1981b] Conditions for transitivity of majority rule with algorithmic interpretations. Technical Report 347, Center for Research on Organizational Efficiency, Institute for Mathematical Studies in the Social Sciences, Encina Hall, Stanford University.

Raynaud, H. [1981c] How restrictive actually are the value restriction conditions. Technical Report 348, Center for Research on Organizational Efficiency, Institute for Mathematical Studies in the Social Sciences, Encina Hall, Stanford University.

Raynaud, H. [1982] The individual freedom allowed by the value restriction conditions. Technical Report 360, Center for Research in Organizational Efficiency, Institute for Mathematical Studies in the Social Sciences, Encina Hall, Stanford University.

Romero, D. [1978] *Variations sur l'Effet Condorcet.* Thesis of the 3rd Cycle, Université Scientifique et Médicale de Grenoble (France).

Satterthwaite, M. A. [1975] Strategy-proofness and Arrow's conditions: existence and correspondence theorems for voting procedures and social welfare functions. *Journal of Economic Theory* 10:187–217.

Sen, A. K. [1966] A possibility theorem on majority decisions. *Econometrica* 34:491–499.

Smith, J. H. [1973] Aggregation of preferences with variable electorate. *Econometrica* 41:1027–1042.

Susmann, B., J.-P. Gremy, M. Marc, and P. Buffet [1967] Peut-on choisir en tenant compte de critères multiples? Une méthode (ELECTRE) et trois applications. *Metra* 6:283–316.

Ungar, G. [1973] Evidence for molecular coding of neural information. In H. P. Zippel (ed.) *Memory and Transfer of Information.* New York and London: Plenum, pp. 317–341.

Ward, B. [1965] Majority voting and alternative forms of public enterprise. In J. Margolis (ed.), *Public Economy of Urban Communities.* Baltimore: Johns Hopkins Press, pp. 112–126.

Young, H. P. [1974] An axiomatisation of Borda's rule. *Journal of Economic Theory* 9:43–52.

Young, H. P. [1975] Social choice scoring functions. *Siam Journal of Applied Mathematics* 28:824–838.

Yu, P. L. [1979] Behavior bases and habitual domains of human decision/behavior. In G. Fautel and T. G. Gale (eds.), *Multiple Criteria Decision-Making: Theory and Application.* Heidelberg: Springer-Verlag.

Index

Page number in italics refers to figure

DATE DUE